The Local Church Looks to the Future

LYLE E. SCHALLER

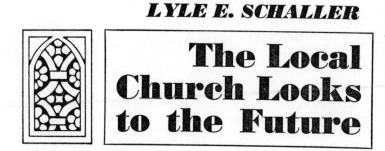

The Local Church Looks to the Future

Abingdon Press ⅌ Nashville and New York

THE LOCAL CHURCH LOOKS TO THE FUTURE

ISBN 0-687-22524-8

Library of Congress Catalog Card Number: 68-17449

Scripture quotations unless otherwise noted are
from the Revised Standard Version of the Bible,
copyright 1946 and 1952 by the Division of
Christian Education, National Council of
Churches, and are used by permission.

Portions of Chapter 5 have been adapted from
articles that originally appeared in *Church
Management,* October and December, 1966, and
January–March, 1967.

SET UP, PRINTED, AND BOUND BY THE
PARTHENON PRESS, AT NASHVILLE,
TENNESSEE, UNITED STATES OF AMERICA

To Dr. and Mrs. Murray H. Leiffer

Contents

Introduction

This book rests on four simple assumptions.

The first, and by far the most important here, is that the local church is neither obsolete nor irrelevant. While not all the necessary ministries needed in contemporary society can be based on the traditional congregational structure of Christianity, this does not mean that the congregation should be abandoned. The congregation and the parish church have been the dominant institutional expressions of the Christian church for nearly two thousand years.

The early disciples went out and founded congregations of the followers of the way. Foreign missionaries learned that they must begin by establishing a ministry of the Word and sacrament as quickly as possible. Students of the growth of the church in South America, Asia, and Africa have concluded that when new congregations are founded, new people are reached with the good news; when this is not done, church growth levels off. The same point has been made by those who have studied new church development in the United States. The historical evidence clearly indicates that the con-

9

gregation is the most effective channel for carrying out the great missionary commandment in Matthew 28:19.

The parish church is still the most important expression of the church, for the parish is the most concrete form of the church for the vast majority of Christians today. It is the door through which they came into a new relationship with God. The parish is still the foundation on which all other tangible expressions of the church are based. It is from the parish church that are drawn the money and the manpower to support and staff the new forms of the church which are viewed by many critics of the parish as the hope of tomorrow. It is the parish church which supplies the money to pay the salaries of many of the critics who contend that the parish church is obsolete, irrelevant, and unnecessary. It is the parish which provides the continuity for the church from generation to generation. Most important of all, it is in and through the local church that individuals come to know Christ, to grow in the faith, to have their lives changed, and to go forth into the world to witness to their faith.

There is no substitute for corporate worship, and there is no substitute for the community of believers in which the Word is preached and the sacraments are duly administered. There is no substitute for the sense and experience of Christian community which can be found only in the parish church. There is no substitute for what the Manifesto adopted by the Lutheran Church in America in 1966 refers to as "the family of God in which those who suffer the bruises of life find support and help, the complacent are stirred and the creative and venturesome are encouraged." The parish church is still the best place from which the church can reach out to people to bring them the good news of Jesus Christ. The parish church is still the best base for reaching out to the various structures and institutions of the world, for many of the men and women who constitute these structures and control these institutions are members of a local church, and this is often the only and certainly the most important contact the church has with them.

So long as the family remains the basic social unit of our society, there will be a place and a need for the parish church which ministers to the family as a family and to the members of the family as individuals. Contrary to critics of the local church who contend that people "no longer live where they live," the vast majority of Americans do lead family-centered lives. This is true is suburbia, it is true in rural America, and it is especially true in the inner city. Thus far no one has discovered a better way of ministering to the family, and to the individual who is the member of a family, than the parish church. Despite the high visibility of the nonfamily individual, 92 percent of the American people do live in family units.

This book is based on the assumption that the congregation as represented by the local church will continue to be the most common institutional expression of the church and that for the vast majority of Americans the institutional link between the individual and the universal church will continue to be the congregation and the parish church.

This is not meant to suggest that other nonparochial ministries are not needed. They are, and they are needed in increasing numbers and greater varieties. Some of these must be issue-centered rather than person-centered ministries. The churches need to be more actively involved in the crucial issues of the day, such as poverty, unemployment, the struggle for social and legal justice, race relations, peace, urban renewal, housing, education, and pollution of the environment. These nonparochial issue-centered ministries provide an opportunity for the churches to become more meaningfully involved in the world. Frequently the most effective means of carrying out these issue-centered ministries is from an ecumenical base involving several denominations, communions, and faiths. This does not mean, however, that contact with the parish should be abandoned. These specialized issue-centered ministries should be thought of as supplementing the parish, not as replacing it.

Some of these specialized nonparochial ministries are person-centered. These include the coffeehouses, some of the shopping center ministries, the growing number of itinerant street ministries, several of the ministries to tourists, and the apartment ministries. While some of these are exploratory and have no future, most of these attempts to supplement the outreach of the parish through specialized ministries are important and will be even more important tomorrow. They should not be regarded as rivals of the parish, however. Many of these specialized nonparochial ministries, especially the person-centered ones, can and should be related to a worshiping congregation where the Word is preached and the sacraments are administered. Experience again demonstrates that unless these specialized ministries are related to a worshiping congregation *or to some institutionalized expression of the church such as the parish,* the church will not be able to fulfill all its responsibilities to the people it seeks to reach and serve, to society, or to Christ.

The second assumption on which this book rests is that all the basic purposes of the local church are compatible with one another. There no inherent theological or religious reason why a parish cannot engage in all facets of "congregational care," including preaching of the Word and administration of the sacraments, and concurrently be an effective vehicle for evangelism *and* engage in mission in the world. It would be heretical to assume that these are incompatible purposes.

On the other hand, it must be recognized that natural institutional pressures may produce goals that are consistent with one or more of these purposes, but which are mutually incompatible. The resulting tensions, however, are a product of these institutional pressures and of flaws in the goal formation process. They are not a result of incompatible purposes.

The third fundamental assumption is that institutionalism is a fact of life in the local church (as in denominational, interdenominational, and ecumenical agencies). Furthermore it is assumed that church leaders can be more helpful and creative by accepting this fact than by a head-in-the-sand rejection of it.

In accepting the fact of institutionalism, a distinction must be drawn between a *religious* institution and other institutions. A local church, while it is an institution and displays many forms of institutional behavior, is different from secular institutions. It is different in terms of purposes, goals, and organization. Most of all it is different in terms of its reason for being, its motivation, and its relationship to God. As a *religious* institution it has a unique role in the world and a unique role in the lives of persons.

This book is concerned with that institutional expression of the church known as the parish or the congregation or the local church. This means that considerations of institutional structure, problems of institutional blight, and the elements of institutional change cannot be neglected. Nevertheless, the fact that the parish is a *religious* institution does mean that the response of churchmen to institutionalism in the parish will be different than the response to institutionalism in other segments of society.

At times the pressures of institutional blight become so great that the parish no longer bears much resemblance to a religious organization. This has happened and is happening to literally thousands of local churches. Anyone who is a true friend of the parish must recognize this and acknowledge it openly. An unknown number of Protestant parishes stand in great need of spiritual renewal. For others it is already too late. To acknowledge the fact and the liabilities of institutionalism, however, does not require one to denounce all institutional expressions of the church. This awareness of the risks and dangers that are inherent in any institution, *including the parish,* should encourage the Christian to be more receptive to the insights that will help him fight the blight that inevitably accompanies institutionalism.

The fourth assumption on which this book rests is that the quality of the decision-making process in the local church can be improved. It is assumed that the decision makers in the parish can benefit by developing a systematic statement of purpose, by carefully formulating a relevant set of goals, and by considering the experiences of other parishes. It is also assumed that "outsiders" can be helpful to leaders in the local church and that these leaders will utilize the assistance of outsiders. This book is intended to be a resource for parish leaders in their planning for the future of their local church. It is an effort to provide help on eight of the most common planning problems facing parish leaders today. The primary purpose is not to be directive, but rather to be provocative. This book is based on firsthand involvement with the experiences of an unknown number of churchmen in over a thousand parishes representing more than a score of denominations in two dozen states.

The contents of the book are based on the experiences of these parishes, and every event, suggestion, recommendation, illustration, and conversation reported in this book are taken from real life, most of them being firsthand reports. A few are comments and experiences relayed to me by clergymen and laymen. Much of the dialogue has been taken from conferences and planning sessions with parish committees. To avoid embarrassing anyone, proper names have been changed, and in a few cases other descriptive data have been altered slightly to conceal identities. The names of all persons and parishes described are fictitious. In some chapters the experiences of two or more parishes or pastors have been combined in the interests of continuity and brevity. For example, the story of Pastor Richard Hanson and St. John's Church in chapter 1 and the experiences of St. Mark's in chapter 5 are actually the sum of the experiences of several different parishes. In other chapters the events in a particular section did occur as described in a single parish. Much of the first part of chapter 4, for example, is an almost literal account of a single meeting that occurred one Tuesday morning.

This book begins with an account of the vital importance of a clear statement of purpose and of some of the tensions that can result from the lack of an understanding by the members of *what* the parish is seeking to do and *why* this is important. Closely related to this is the material in chapter 2 with the emphasis on the goals that grow out of this statement of purpose.

In chapter 3 an attempt is made to discuss the most important problem confronting many parishes, the need to reach out to the people who live in the neighborhood of the parish church but who are outside any church. Evangelism is the most neglected function of most local churches today, and this chapter is an effort to provide some assistance on this vital matter.

The growing vigor of the ecumenical movement has encouraged many church leaders to ask themselves how they can cooperate with other parishes. Two areas of cooperation—cooperative ministries and joint use of buildings—are explored in chapter 4.

Despite the current and widely publicized antibuilding sentiment in American Protestantism, many parishes find themselves confronted with the necessity of going into a building program. They find they cannot do the job unless they have the tools, and the building usually is an essential tool. Anyone who has worked extensively with inner city congregations can testify to the validity of this statement. Perhaps the easiest way to discover the value of an adequate building in carrying out the mission of the local church is to work with an inner city congregation that has been meeting in a storefront for several years. In chapter 5 are discussed five of the major aspects of an effective building program.

In chapter 6 a special, but comparatively common, type of local church planning problem is reviewed, and generalizations from experience are offered for the use of those who wonder what is ahead for the downtown church or for old First Church.

What's ahead for our church? In many cases an honest answer to that question is simply nothing. During the next decade thousands of local churches will disappear from the scene through dissolution, merger, or relocation. A large proportion of these are located in rural America, but a sizable minority are in urban and suburban communities. Some will be forced to terminate their existence because of urban renewal and highway projects. A far larger number will disappear as a result of population movements and economic trends. Others are simply too small to continue to function as separate organizations in a complex society which is built around a cash economy and demands a high level of formal education in its professional leadership. The economic costs, the shortage of pastors, and the ease of private transportation combine to make the closing of thousands of small parishes an inevitable part of the future. Another larger group will disappear as a result of the merger of the parent denominations. The merger of the Evangelical and Reformed Church with the Congregational Christian Church already has resulted in the elimination of many parishes—usually through mergers. The merger of the Evangelical United Brethren Church and The Methodist Church may result in the elimination during the next few decades of hundreds of what are now separate local churches. Some of the issues and questions raised by these facts are discussed in chapter 7.

For many church leaders the most difficult question is one of effecting change. In chapter 8 a case study is presented to illustrate an outline or strategy for achieving change that is both simple and effective.

It should be clear to every reader that this book, far most than most, rests upon the contributions of many different people. I am deeply grateful to the pastors, laymen, and denominational staff persons who have shared with me their experiences and insights. I am thankful for the opportunity to have had firsthand encounters with a couple of hundred parishes each year for the past several years. (One of the lessons I have learned from these contacts with many different local churches is that while many of the faults and shortcomings of the parish church tend to have a very high degree of visibility, most of the accomplishments and achievements tend to have a very low degree of visibility. This may be a result of the nature of the church. This distinction in visibility means that the local church tends to produce ammunition for the guns of the critics of the parish without providing equivalent support for those who affirm the validity and value of the parish.) I also am greatly indebted to the trustees of the Regional Church Planning Office who have made it possible for me to have these opportunities to become involved in the life and ministry of these parishes.

I owe a special word of thanks to Jean Bergold, George H. Brown, Shirley Regis, and Richard L. Ruggles. These four persons literally gave me the freedom, the energy, and the time to turn a stack of file folders into the manuscript that became this book.

Part of chapter 5 appeared as copyrighted articles in *Church Management* in 1966 and 1967, and I am grateful to the publisher, Norman Hersey, for permission to reprint portions of those articles.

This book is dedicated to two longtime servants, friends, and supporters of the parish church who have guided, goaded, inspired, and helped me in many different ways during the years. I am grateful for their interest, their wisdom, and, most of all, for their friendship.

LYLE E. SCHALLER

1

What Is Our Purpose?

"Pastor, it has been over a year since you were out to see me. Dr. Franklin used to stop in every few weeks when he was our minister." These words were spoken by a tiny, white-haired widow as she stopped at the door to shake hands with her pastor at St. John's Church.

"Thanks for reminding me," smiled the Reverend Mr. Richard Hanson. "I'll stop by the first chance I get, and we'll have a good visit. It may not be for awhile though," he warned. "You know we're pretty busy trying to strengthen the church's outreach in this community."

THE GLORIFICATION OF THE WORM — HOWARD HENDRICKS

The minister continued to greet his flock as they filed past him. He exchanged brief pleasantries with most of them and made mental notes as he was told of a member who was entering the hospital on Monday, that a light bulb was burned out in the ladies' rest room, that the Greens wanted their baby baptized the second Sunday of the next month, that his salary check would be several days late because the treasurer had been called out of town unexpectedly and had not signed any checks before leaving, and that the Grahams expected their son Tim to arrive home Thursday after a tour of duty with the army in Vietnam.

The last person to shake his hand that morning was Mrs. Rogers, a tall, stately woman whose late husband had been one of the pillars of the church for over thirty years. "Good morning, Pastor," she said. "I hear you now have nearly one hundred young people coming out for this new Sunday evening program you started last fall. Is that true?"

"Yes, it is true," he replied with a heartfelt smile. "Our attendance actually averages about seventy to eighty, but there are over one hundred young people involved." As he offered this response, Pastor Hanson felt a sense of delight that one of the "old guard" recognized what an effort was involved in developing a program that could attract one hundred senior high youngsters. This warm glow suddenly disappeared when Mrs. Rogers dropped his hand with the comment, "Hrumpf, if you have one hundred teen-agers in this Sunday evening affair, you must be letting in a lot of outsiders! There aren't more than thirty or forty young people that age in this congregation."

As Mrs. Rogers swept on out to the parking lot, Dick Hanson asked himself for the hundredth time, "What am I doing here?" Three years earlier he had accepted a call to St. John's. His first two pastorates after graduating from seminary had been in stable churches in smaller cities, and, while he felt he had served acceptably in both of them, after twelve years in the ministry he was ready for a new challenge when the call came from St. John's.

St. John's was the third oldest Protestant church in the

state capital and for decades had been one of the leading churches in the synod. The membership had dropped from over 1,500 back in the 1920's to a reported 485 forty years later. Some of the old-timers claimed they used to have over a thousand persons in Sunday school every Sunday. Now the Sunday school attendance averaged fewer than one hundred.

The pulpit committee had been very frank about these facts; they had described the changes that had taken place in the neighborhood during the past few years. The church was located in one of the oldest residential neighborhoods in the city, and many of the old large homes had been converted into rooming houses or apartment houses. The church was in the center of the neighborhood, about one mile from the central business district and on a major traffic artery. The chairman of the pulpit committee had been very specific in his comments to Dick. "We're looking for a minister who has had ten to fifteen years' experience, but who is young enough in age and spirit to lead us in mission in this neighborhood. Many of our members are getting along in years; most of them no longer live in this neighborhood, but they all love St. John's. They all want to see St. John's provide the ministry that is needed in this neighborhood. We all realize that this won't happen unless we have the right kind of ministerial leadership. Unless a man can see the vision and is eager to accept this challenge, we don't want him!"

Mr. Rogers, who died three weeks after Dick Hanson accepted the call to St. John's, was a member of that pulpit committee. Dick remembered his saying, "We want a minister who can come in and build up this congregation to what it used to be. There are hundreds of unchurched people living in this neighborhood. St. John's needs to go out and reach them."

Dick also recalled another member adding, "There's a lot of potential in our own congregation. If the minister would get out and call among the members and stir them up, they would attend more often and be more active. This church has a lot of good people in it—all we need is the right kind of leadership."

After visiting the church and two more meetings with the pulpit committee Dick Hanson decided this was the challenge he had been seeking and accepted the call to St. John's. The first year had been the traditional honeymoon period as he called on all the members, became acquainted with the leaders of the parish, and talked about the possibilities of serving the neighborhood.

Shortly before the beginning of the second year, he had outlined to the church council a new program directed toward neighborhood residents. The council had given its enthusiastic approval and in three weeks had raised the extra $4,600 he suggested was needed to carry out the program. Most of the money was allocated for the salary of a seminary student who would be full-time during the summer and would help on weekends during the school year with the youth program.

Now, after three years, what was the result? As he asked himself this question, Pastor Hanson thought perhaps it was all symbolized in a recent incident that involved the new sign in front of the church. Back in the middle of his first year as pastor, Dick had casually remarked one evening at church council that a stranger would not know what kind of church this was or the time of service. Sometime earlier during a clean-up campaign the old decrepit sign in the yard of the church had been torn down and never replaced. Six weeks after the new pastor had dropped his casual hint, a new illuminated masonry sign costing $2,000 was under construction, and every nickel of the cost was in the treasurer's hands as the result of a quiet fund-raising drive conducted by two of the men on the council.

Last Tuesday evening the synod missions executive had come to meet with the congregation. He had arrived early, and since it was a warm evening, he had stood out in front talking with a couple of the members he had known for years. While they talked, one of the ladies exclaimed, "Look at those kids climbing all over the church sign! They shouldn't be allowed to do that. Why, there's even one crawling into the fellowship hall through a window! I don't know what's going to happen here." Turning to the synod mission executive, she continued, "I guess now you can see why a lot of us are unhappy at how things have been going here for the past several months."

"I think I know what you mean," responded the denominational executive, "but it seems to me this is a sign of progress. I've been coming here at least once a year for nearly a decade now, and this is the first time I have seen a youngster anywhere near the church. This is progress!"

Later when he heard this story, Dick Hanson said to the synod official, "This illustrates my frustrations. When I accepted a call here, it was with the clear-cut understanding that St. John's would make a major effort to serve the people living in this neighborhood. Everyone gave verbal approval to the idea. During the past two years we have reached a lot of people in the neighborhood, especially kids. So what is the result? I am criticized because I don't call in the homes of the members. The people from the neighborhood who come near the building are made to feel like they are intruders or vandals. The church treasurer has warned me that the money probably won't be available next year to hire a part-time seminary student; yet plans are moving ahead to raise $30,000 to replace the old organ. Several people have gone out of their way to point out that while we are in contact with many neighborhood residents, only a few have joined the church, and none of them are good supporters of the budget. I hear a lot more about the cost of replacing a few broken windows and repairing a couple of tables than I do about the number of youth in our Sunday evening fellowship group.

"Everyone continues to say that they want the church to serve this neighborhood," continued the pastor, "but most of them are unwilling to accept the consequences of this decision. I can't help wondering if I have made a mistake in the way I have acted. The tension is so thick in this church that you can cut it with a knife. This shouldn't be. A parish that is doing the Lord's work ought not to be torn by dissension the way this one is!"

"You're right," agreed the synod executive. "When a parish is doing what it should be doing, there ought not to be the tension and conflict you describe. Yet your situation is not at all uncommon, especially in a gathered congregation such as this one. Any attempt by a gathered congregation to initiate a new ministry into the neighborhood almost invariably places the pastor in a tension-producing dilemma. The larger and the stronger this gathered congregation, the greater the tension."

"But this shouldn't be!" protested Pastor Hanson. "When a parish is faithful and obedient to the Lord's will, there should be peace, not conflict!"

"Perhaps you're right, Dick," responded the synod official. "Sometimes I think that when we see the kind of tension you say is present here at St. John's, this suggests that a heretical definition of the church is governing the actions and attitudes of the members.

"Possibly I am to blame for some of your problems here," he continued. "When Dr. Franklin suddenly resigned because of his health, I met with members of this congregation on several occasions. A few wanted to relocate, but most of them felt they should stay. When they asked my opinion, I urged them to stay and to look forward to developing a strong neighborhood-oriented ministry. I suggested they look for a young, experienced pastor who had maturity, imagination, vision, and energy. I was delighted when they decided to call you.

"Where I made my mistake was in not spending more time with them talking through this question of the purpose of the church. I assumed that they knew what the church is supposed to be and that this was not necessary. It appears that I did both you and the congregation a disservice by my neglect."

"Maybe it's not too late," interrupted Dick Hanson. "Maybe all of us here at St. John's should ask you to come in and help us work on this question of the purpose of the church. This might be a good time for us to go through this experience. By doing this now, rather than three years ago, it may have more meaning. Now we can look at the implications of what we say rather than simply repeat a few clichés. Do you ever do this with parishes such as ours? What kind of outline do you use? Maybe you could give us an outline of what we should do, and we can follow through the process without using up your time."

As Dick Hanson and the synod executive continued their conversation, it became apparent that they were discussing two different, but closely related, problems at St. John's. The more highly visible one was the dissension in the parish and the growing tension produced by the effort to develop an effective neighborhood-oriented ministry.

The second problem at St. John's, and perhaps the basic cause of the first, was the lack of a clearly defined purpose. The members had not been challenged to think carefully through the reasons for St. John's existence. Many did not see the relationship of this new effort to serve the neighborhood to the rest of the church program.

St. John's is not alone in being confronted with these two related problems. They are very common in Protestant parishes today. Both are disruptive and can greatly inhibit the effectiveness of the local church. Both are often neglected and eventually may develop into fatal illnesses. They merit closer examination here.

The Sources of Tension over Purpose

At St. John's, as happens so often in similar situations, the decision to undertake a new neighborhood-oriented ministry places the minister unexpectedly in a tension-filled dilemma. He finds himself caught between the expectations of those who believe the pastor should minister to his flock and those who have caught the new vision of the church's ministry to the world. He sees the results of the new effort measured by contradictory standards of evaluation. Some members appear to be more interested in preserving the building than in saving souls. Others resent any program which appears to overlook the members or the children of members. Many evaluate any new venture solely on the basis of the number of new members received or by the effect on the treasurer's report.

As Pastor Hanson struggled with this at St. John's, it is not surprising that he moved toward the conclusion that the tension in his parish was the product of incompatible purposes. He began to question whether it is possible for a gathered congregation to be in mission to the world without this producing destructive internal conflicts in the life of the parish.

The most helpful way to analyze this question is to examine the *source* of the tension. The source of the tension at St. John's was *not within* the definition of what the church is or of what the church should be doing. The source of the tension at St. John's was a result of the lack of a clear understanding of the purpose of the church. Many of the members acted on the assumption that the local church should direct its efforts toward serving the members. This meant that the pastor should be concerned *primarily* with ministering to the members. "After all, we pay his salary. Why shouldn't he be expected to give first priority to the wants and needs of the members?" They defined the purpose of the church strictly in terms of a ministry to the gathered congregation.

Others recognized the need for the church to reach out and serve the newcomers to the neighborhood around the church building. It appeared, however, that these members hoped this could be accomplished without making any changes at St. John's. They appeared to expect that somehow the newcomers would happily fit into the traditional pattern of the operation at St. John's. They really were not so much interested in reaching the unchurched with the gospel as they were in finding replacements for the members who died or moved away. Their real definition of the purpose was centered on the need for the institution to perpetuate itself.

Another group sincerely wanted the newcomers to the neighborhood to come to St. John's, but they felt that the responsibility for this rested on the new residents, not on the members at St. John's. "Our door is wide open; we have plenty of room, and these people know they are welcome. If they want the church, all they have to do is to walk in." These people appeared to define the purpose of the church as merely to be present and available to those outside it. Their definition of purpose did not include any responsibility for the members to engage themselves actively in outreach and evangelism.

A few of the leaders, including those who had served on the pulpit committee three years earlier, recognized that St. John's must attempt to reach the people living around the church. They saw this as an essential element in the definition of purpose. Unfortunately, however, they placed too much responsibility for the communication and execution of this on the new pastor and too little on the members.

The result was that the more effort Pastor Hanson put into doing what he believed he had been called to do and what he believed he should be doing, the greater the tension in the parish. The primary source of this tension was the failure of the members to have a common understanding of the purpose or reason for the existence of their church. Without this common understanding it was impossible to develop a strategy for the parish, or even to agree on how the pastor should spend his time.

Closely related to the first source was the second source of tension. This was the lack of adequate lines of communication within the congregation which would enable the members to understand the purpose, to share in the development of a strategy for fulfilling that purpose, and to know what their church was doing and why. In many parishes this is something of a chicken and egg question. Which comes first? Open up channels of internal communication? Or develop ideas, proposals, plans, strategies, and activities to feed into these channels? Perhaps the best answer is both. As the members, and especially the leaders, grapple with these questions of purpose, strategy, and program development, there is a need to communicate what is happening to other members of the parish simultaneously. The best method of communication, of course, is participation and involvement. While this is not the primary reason, it is a very important reason for maximizing the number of people who are involved in these discussions.

A third source of tension in many parishes also grows out of this question of purpose. This is the tension that is created by a conflict between what the Lord is calling the church to do and what some members would like to see their church be. The tension is produced by the difference between God's call and man's wants. For example, one can find parishes in which a few members are attempting to manipulate the purpose and program of a parish for their own self-gratification. This may create some very severe tensions in the congregation. Sometimes we see members adopt worldly standards to measure the "success" of their church. They want to evaluate their church by the prestige of the members, the rate of growth, the size of the budget, the amount of the endowment, or the splendor of the building. When such standards of evaluation are applied, this will produce almost inevitably a distorted sense of purpose.

To recognize that the source of this tension in the parish is the lack of a common understanding of the purpose of the church is an important first step toward reducing the tension. It is not possible to take any additional steps, however, without defining the purpose of the local church.

An Outline for Defining Purpose

The members of each parish must make the effort to discover and articulate the purpose of their church for themselves. They can and should turn to the New Testament for the foundation on which to build their own statement of purpose. They can turn to a creed for a generalized statement; from this they can move into a specific and detailed statement of the purpose of their own church in this community at this point in history. They may be able to use an outline developed by another parish as a guide for their thinking. They must, however, develop the detailed statement of purpose for their parish by themselves. This should be related to both the biblical concept of the church and to the needs of the people in the community in which their church is located. This statement of purpose also should be in a form which is helpful in guiding the development of a strategy, which can be communicated to all the members and which also can be used in self-evaluation. Finally, it should be a balanced statement which does not overemphasize certain facets of purpose while neglecting others.

A simplified outline which meets all of these requirements can be built around three points.

1. *Congregational Care*

Here are grouped those items which are entirely or largely member-oriented. Typically this includes corporate worship, administration of the sacraments, pastoral care, fellowship, and the nurture, education, and training for Christian discipleship of the members.

2. *Outreach and Evangelism*

This part of the statement focuses on the imperative to go out and confront individuals outside the church with the good news that Jesus Christ is their Redeemer and Savior. While the first part of this outline was directed toward the parish's ministry to persons inside the gathered community, this part of the outline emphasizes the parish's responsibility to *individuals outside* the church.

3. *Witness and Mission*

The emphasis here is on the church's responsibility to be a living witness to Christ in the world to the groups, organizations, structures, and institutions outside the church in the world. This also helps the members to understand both the legitimacy and the imperative for the parish's involvement in the social, economic, and political issues in the local community. In part two of this outline the thrust is on christianizing the world; in this part the emphasis is on humanizing the society in which man lives.

A parish planning committee can use this basic outline to develop a more detailed statement of the purpose of their church. They can use this as a basis for developing a plan of action or strategy. This same outline also can be used as a frame of reference for helping all the members arrive at a common understanding of the purpose of their church. It can be used as the outline for communicating to all the members what their church is doing and why. This three-point outline also can be used to submit to the members a "performance budget" of the church's expenditures. Instead of presenting a budget or a record of expenditures using the traditional categories of salaries, utilities, etc., these three categories are used. Instead of placing the emphasis on "input," as is done in the traditional budget, the emphasis is placed on "output" or results or program. This enables the members to see the results of the dollar input into their parish. This type of outline of purpose also encourages members to give the appropriate emphasis to all elements of purpose.

The Importance of a Balanced Definition

This matter of a *balanced* statement of purpose is sometimes overlooked when a parish begins to develop a strategy for mission. If the strategy is to be biblically sound, internally consistent, and relevant to the contemporary situation, it must be based on a balanced definition of purpose. This point was emphasized by the synod mission executive as he talked with

Dick Hanson. The two men had discussed the sources of tension at St. John's and talked about the necessity of the members going through the process of developing their own statement of purpose.

At this point the synod executive moved on to stress the importance of a balanced definition. "Let's take this first point of congregational care," he said. "Most church members have no difficulty accepting this as a purpose of the church. They can see the importance of providing the opportunity for members to gather together for worship and the administration of the sacraments. They can see the role of the church in the education and nurture of the members. They know they want the pastoral care provided by the minister. They recognize the need for members to come to know and love one another and for the congregation to develop a sense of community. Now all this is a very important part of the definition of purpose, and I can see and understand why a congregation may devote 50 or 60 or 70 or perhaps in a few parishes even as much as 80 percent of all its efforts and resources toward fulfilling this one basic purpose in terms of member-oriented functions and activities; but too often I find congregations in which the leaders see this as the *only* purpose of the local church.

"On the other hand many of the critics of the parish today, especially some clergymen in nonparochial positions, are highly critical of this idea of congregational care and member-oriented programming as the major purpose of the local church. They contend that the emphasis should be on the church in mission in the world.

"I believe there is a middle ground here," continued the

synod executive, "and I think I can help a congregation see the legitimacy of congregational care *and* the necessity of mission and witness *and* the need for evangelistic outreach to the unchurched. The danger we run into is that a congregation overemphasizes one and neglects the other two. This can kill the church. We have had literally hundreds of Protestant parishes commit suicide by overemphasizing this matter of congregational care. They become so wrapped up in themselves that they completely, or almost completely, neglect the second and third parts of this threefold definition—evangelism and mission. Usually what happens is that this shift in emphasis occurs so gradually that no one realizes it until long after it has happened and the parish is no longer a *religious* institution but simply another institution concerned with the institutional goals of self-preservation and institutional maintenance. Churches that drift off into this distorted definition of purpose may continue to exist long after they have died as *religious* institutions. They can exist on the accumulated assets from the past from building, endowment, loyalty, tradition, and habit. They cannot witness and reach out effectively without the current income that comes only from faith, obedience to the call of the Lord, participation in the world, and love of neighbor."

"As the pastor of this church, I certainly can see how a parish can die because of overemphasis on what you describe as congregational care and concern for preserving the institution. Jesus' comment about what happens to him who seeks to save his own life certainly applies to the church also," remarked Dick Hanson. "Now are you also suggesting that a parish may get into trouble by overemphasizing evangelism and mission?"

"Well, we've had at least three churches in this synod during the past dozen years that were dissolved because too much emphasis was placed on mission and witness while too little effort was devoted to the needs and care of the members," replied the denominational official. "I must confess, however, that I have never heard of a parish getting into trouble because an excessive proportion of its resources was devoted to evangelism. In my opinion evangelism is the most severely neglected purpose in our mainline Protestant churches today. I don't think we need to worry about placing too much emphasis on evangelism."

"I find it a little hard to believe that a church could put so much emphasis on mission and witness that this could kill the church or cause it to dissolve," commented Pastor Hanson.

"Well, I'm convinced that this is precisely what happened in three congregations in our synod," replied the synod missions executive. "Sometimes we hear and read so much about the need for the local church to do this or to do that to prove that it is in mission that we forget this matter of balance. It's not enough to try to humanize society; we also must evangelize the unchurched individuals in the world. Some church members need the opportunity the church provides to carry out a ministry in the world, others need to be ministered to, some members need the opportunity to serve, and some need to be served. Most congregations include some of each, and many people do move from one category to another at different times. The proportion of those who have the resources to minister and of those who need to be ministered to varies from parish to parish and from time to time. In one of our churches the number of members who were too old, too tired, or too insecure to go out and minister was increasing, and the number with the capacity and the desire to be in mission was declining. Each of the last three pastors to serve that parish kept challenging the congregation to be in mission, and each one severely neglected the congregational care function. The members of that parish needed to be challenged with the call to the church to be in mission in the world; but the members also needed to be loved. They needed to be inspired and renewed by the celebration of the resurrection of Jesus. They needed to be helped in overcoming their own selfishness. This did not happen, and the parish died from spiritual malnutrition because of an imbalance in the definition of purpose."

"You're almost saying that we can overemphasize this concept of mission and servanthood if I hear you correctly," commented Dick Hanson.

"Not exactly," replied the synod official. "What I am pleading for is a balanced definition of the purpose of the church and of the role of the individual Christian. Maybe that does mean that I am saying we sometimes romanticize the idea of mission and that we overemphasize this one facet of the definition of purpose, but what I really mean is that we should not neglect other vital elements of a complete definition of purpose. Take this matter of servanthood, for example. The concept of the servant church has received great emphasis recently. But remember what Jesus said as recorded in John 15:15: 'No longer do I call you servants, for the servant does not know what his master is doing; but I have called you friends, for all that I have heard from my Father I have made known to you.' We need to move from this very provocative and inspiring concept of servanthood to the concept of friendship. Among other things, this says to me that the pastor and members of a parish should minister to one another, not only as faithful and obedient servants, but also as friends. If the pastor and the members can relate to one another as friends, as well as fellow servants, this will eliminate many of the tensions that often handicap our local churches so greatly."

"Are you preaching to me?" asked Pastor Hanson. "If you are, I think you have just struck home. Perhaps part of the trouble here at St. John's is that I have tried too hard to be a servant, a prophet, a leader, and a pastor, but I have not worked hard enough at being a friend."

"I don't know enough about your situation here to comment on that; you know better than I what the answer is to your question," replied the synod official. "All I am trying to say is that church members are people too, and we should love them and treat them as friends. In other words, if you feel compelled to challenge the people to change and to accept new ideas, don't smear it in their faces. Help them to overcome their reluctance, their natural rebellion, and their feeling of being threatened. Instead of feeling like a martyred servant, think of yourself as a friend, as an enabler who helps the congregation move to accepting and fulfilling its purpose as a church."

Change and the Reaction to Change

"Perhaps I am sounding impatient again," said Dick Hanson, "but how long does this take? I've been here at St. John's for three years now. When I accepted the call to come here, I thought they already had made up their mind that they wanted to develop a strong, neighborhood-oriented ministry. During my first year I spent most of my time getting to know the members and giving them the chance to get to know me. We seemed to be in complete agreement about the purpose of this church—the need for this church to focus its energies on this neighborhood and to orient a program to the residents of this area. Yet when we actually move in this direction and do accomplish something, we arouse a hostile reaction in many of the members. The more progress we make, the greater the tension."

"This is neither surprising nor unusual, but I understand how it can be very frustrating," was the reply. "In responding to these reactions, you have to keep in mind that change is threatening, especially to many older people. While the people here at St. John's probably would never put it in these terms, what they have been saying to you for the past three years is that we want to change, we want to adapt our program to a changing neighborhood, we want to achieve the goal of being a relevant church in this neighborhood, but *we want to stay the same as we are*. During your first year, when the goals of change were articulated and idealized but no changes were taking place, this did not produce any serious strains. As soon as you actually started to implement a program to achieve these goals, you confronted the members with the fact of change. For some this is certain to be threatening. This creates tension. This is one reason why, as I tried to point out earlier, it is important for the members to have a solid understanding of the purpose of the church. This will help them cope with change and understand *why* change is necessary. When they understand *why* change is necessary, it isn't as threatening. This takes time.

"A second part of this is that a clear understanding of the purpose of the church, of the concept of servanthood, and of the ministry of the laity will help them recognize that this is a two-way street. As they seek to minister to the people in this neighborhood, they must be open and receptive to the idea that they will be ministered unto at the same time. True ministry involves mutuality. They must come to the realization that the other person has something to offer them also. This requires participation, and it takes time. It takes time to enlarge the number of your people who are involved in this ministry, and it takes time for them to grasp this concept of mutuality. We've learned that the old paternalistic carry-thy-poor-brother's-burden concept doesn't work. We have to treat our poor brother as our equal and realize that he is also helping us carry some of our burdens. Once people discover and understand this idea of brotherhood, of the interdependence of all God's children, many of the tensions you described earlier will vanish.

"Another part of the answer to your question about how long this takes concerns our view of life and of the church. Instead of eagerly looking ahead to a specific day when all the people who call themselves Christian will have a clear-cut understanding of what it means to be a disciple of Christ and a member of his church, I find it more helpful to think of this as a pilgrimage. As we move along, some people drop out of the journey, and new faces join us. We are growing in understanding, but this is a continuing process without a clearly defined terminal point. Hopefully a parish keeps moving ahead and gaining a clearer awareness of its purpose, but pastors come and go, and no one of them can be assured that during his tenure every member will develop a perfect understanding of his role as a Christian or of the purpose of the church."

"Does this mean I'll experience frustration as long as I remain in the pastorate?" asked Dick Hanson. "Are you saying that every church I'll serve will be subject to some tension over purpose? Are you telling me that every pastor and parish is affected by the same tensions and conflict over purpose that plague us here at St. John's?"

"That's about right," replied the synod official. "The only exception I know of is in those parishes where everyone, including the minister, has accepted a narrow definition of purpose that is centered almost entirely around this item of congregational care. Fortunately there aren't many of these left. In most parishes the only real difference is one of degree. If you will think back over your experiences in your other two parishes, I am sure you can recall some differences of opinion among the members over the purpose and role of the church in the world today. These differences of opinion are present in nearly every parish, and these differences create tensions. In some parishes the differences are minor, and the tension is barely noticeable. In other parishes the differences are great, and the tension is very apparent. Some ministers can't stand the pressures produced by these tensions, and others grow impatient when they see that this is a long pilgrimage without an end. These are two of the most common reasons for ministers leaving the pastorate.

"Another point that comes to mind when you ask how long does it take for a congregation to accept the necessity of change," continued the synod executive, "is what I call the 'reaction lag.' This is the period of time between when a congregation is first confronted with a challenge and when it is willing and able to discuss this challenge. Frequently this is a period of three, four, or five years. Often what happens is that the congregation first considers, and then rejects, what turns out to be the eventual, proper course of action. I guess the best biblical parallel I can offer to illustrate my point is the story of Jonah. I have often thought there is a close resemblance between Jonah's rebellion against the will of God and the reluctance of many parishes to face up to the implications of change.

"We see this same pattern in parishes that have to relocate to a larger site in order to accommodate a growing congregation. The first time they consider relocation, they reject it in favor of a proposal to remain at the old location and enlarge the building. Sometimes they have plans prepared and then change their minds; sometimes they actually remodel and enlarge the building, and then vote to move. Likewise when a white congregation is first confronted with the challenge of racial integration, the first response often is a negative one. Later, after the passage of time, the congregation may receive nonwhite members and become an integrated church. Some of the congregations in our synod which today are truly integrated followed this sequence. We see this same pattern of rejection, delay, and then acceptance of a new course of action in many parishes which have been confronted with the need for new buildings, for major changes in program, or for additions to the staff. It is also a very common part of the pre-merger process in the history of churches that enter into mergers. It appears that before a congregation can accept radical change, it frequently must go through the process of rejecting the idea, and then, after the passage of sufficient time, it is free to adopt and implement the proposal."

"Perhaps this is part of the problem here at St. John's," commented Dick Hanson. "The people here never had this period of adjustment between rejection and acceptance of the proposal for a change in the orientation of this church."

"Possibly that is a factor," responded the synod official, "but also remember that the shift from the day when St. John's was a church with a strong neighborhood orientation to the time when it became almost completely a commuter congregation with practically no members living in the neighborhood took place over a period of about twenty-five years. Don't expect to reverse that pattern completely in three years. As long as you're moving in the right direction and as long as you're making progress, there is hope."

"I guess that is consistent with your concept of a pilgrimage," replied Pastor Hanson. "But it surely can be frustrating when most of the people on the pilgrimage either want to sit and rest or else turn around and head back toward the starting point!"

2

What Are Our Goals?

"We've spent six weeks carefully preparing a statement of purpose. I think everyone on the committee that developed this statement of purpose would agree that this has been a valuable experience. Each one of us gained a deeper understanding of the biblical nature of the church, and we certainly came out of this with a new understanding of the role of this church in this community today. I certainly don't regret the time and effort that I put into this, but I have a very practical question. Now that we have agreed on a statement of purpose for this parish, what do we do with it?"

This is a very important question. It is a legitimate question. It is a question frequently asked by persons who have been asked to help state the purpose of their church. It is a question that deserves an answer.

The answer comes in three parts. The first is that this definition of purpose should influence the actions and attitudes of every person in the congregation. It should guide the vote of every decision maker in the parish. This statement of purpose should be the yardstick against which every program, proposal, and allocation of resources must be measured. The larger the number of people who have a meaningful part in the preparation of this statement, the more likely it is that this will happen.

The second part of the answer to this question is that this thoughtfully defined statement of purpose should be the basis for program planning in the parish. So corporate worship was defined as a central element of purpose? What does this mean specifically in terms of a program? How is the program being planned to make this experience of corporate worship more meaningful? What is being done to maximize the number of persons who will have the opportunity to share in corporate worship? What is being done to help people be participants rather than observers in the worship services?

The statement of purpose should be the foundation on which the program is built. It should inspire new and creative ventures in programming. The statement of purpose also should be the basis for evaluating all activities and all program elements of the parish.

At about this point someone may ask, "Now, specifically, what do you mean by these fine sounding sentences? How do you do what you suggest should be done here? How do you translate clichés into clear-cut guidelines?"

These are fair questions, and they lead into the third part of the answer to the earlier question about the usefulness of a statement of purpose.

The preparation of a statement of purpose must be followed by the formulation of a set of goals if the congregation is to receive the maximum return for the investment of time and effort that went into the preparation of that statement.

This idea of goals is not a new one to Christians. Jesus offered many specific goals to his followers. Paul was even more directive in his letters to the new churches.

Another example of the use of goals can be found in the questions that have been asked of every Methodist preacher who seeks to become a full member of an annual conference. These questions were formulated by John Wesley, and many specifically ask about goals. "Are you going on to perfection?" "Do you expect to be made perfect in love in this life?" "Are you earnestly striving after it?" "Are you resolved to devote yourself wholly to God and his work?" "Will you visit from house to house?" "Will you . . . be diligent?" "Will you . . . be punctual?"

The formulation of a set of goals is the best way to turn dreams into reality. This is true of individuals and organizations. It is especially important for voluntary organizations which do not have the benefit of other tools for translating purpose into performance. Before looking specifically at why goals are valuable, it may be helpful to review quickly how goals can be used in developing a program out of the statement of purpose.

From Purpose to Program to Performance

After the statement of the purpose of the parish has been prepared, the next step in the development of a strategy or plan of action is to plan a program. From purpose to program to performance is perhaps the simplest way of describing this process of developing and implementing a strategy for the local church.

Goals can be very useful in this process. First of all, specific goals can help clarify the statement of purpose. The statement of purpose, formulated by the committee mentioned earlier, called for the nurture, education, and training of the members as Christian disciples. One way to begin to turn this ideal into reality is to set a goal of involving sixty members in eight different Bible study groups in which the participants study how the Bible speaks to them today about their problems, their needs, and their obligations as Christians.

A second way goals can be useful in this process is through the development of both short-term *and* long-term goals. For example, the function of evangelism was mentioned in the statement of purpose. The programmatic response was to develop a system of visitation evangelism. In moving from purpose to program to performance it may be helpful to set a short-term goal of calling at every home within a short distance of the church within the next six months. The long-term goal may be to have members call at every home within the geographical parish at least once every two years.

Any discussion of short-term and long-term goals raises the question of deadlines. While some people shy away from the pressures of deadlines, it has been found that deadlines are an essential element in the formulation of short-term and long-term goals. The use of deadlines is also consistent with the New Testament imperative of "Now!"

A third way goals may be helpful at this point in parish planning is in the allocation of resources for program development and execution. In carrying out its avowed purpose of evangelism, one church established the goal of receiving one hundred new members each year. This was helpful because it quantified that goal in terms that people could understand. The leaders could comprehend the amount of resources, especially manpower, that should be allocated to that part of the total program if the goal was to be achieved. They could see that this must be given a very high priority if the performance was to match the expectations expressed by the goal.

This same church soon realized a fourth benefit inherent in the use of goals. This is in the evaluation of performance. In this parish goals were delineated with care and then were used to measure progress. After the first year, when less than sixty new members had been received, it became apparent that either more emphasis must be placed on evangelism or the goal would not be achieved. At the end of the third year the goal of one hundred new members per year had been reached.

Instead of being content that they had achieved the proper balance between the allocation of resources and the goal, the evangelism committee then went back to review what had happened. They discovered that nearly one half of the members received in the first two years had lapsed into inactivity shortly after being received into membership. They saw that their basic goal must be revised to place more emphasis on the assimilation of new members into the life of the fellowship. The new goal became one of receiving *and assimilating* one hundred new members annually. This improvement in the statement of the goal produced an improvement in performance. It is doubtful that this would have happened unless these leaders had been using quantified goals which stimulated the process of evaluation.

It is difficult to place too much emphasis on the value of goals as a means of measuring performance. This is the best method of self-evaluation in a parish. If the program is consistent with the statement of purpose and if the goals are relevant to both, they provide a simple, clear, and effective method of evaluating performance.

A fifth important value of goals is that the formulation *and the achievement of goals* can be extremely useful in conveying a sense of progress. A common affliction of local churches is that members often feel "we're just sitting here spinning our wheels. This church isn't doing anything." Too often they feel this way because their parish is *not* doing anything. Goals can be helpful in curing this malady. More often, however, the parish is active and things are happening, but few realize it. The formulation of goals, the achievement of the goals, and *the communication of this fact to the members* can help them understand which way the parish is headed and how fast it is moving in that direction. Perhaps the most common illustration of this use of goals is in financial campaigns. A vertical bar graph or "thermometer" may be prepared and displayed in the narthex of the church. The top of the bar represents the goal. Each week the vertical bar is colored to show the total progress, and perhaps the progress achieved during the past week, in achieving that goal.

This leads into a sixth, and one of the most important, use of goals, which is the matter of internal communication, especially concerning purpose. Many members do not understand *what* their church is trying to do, and an even larger number probably would have difficulty if they were asked to explain *why*. Goals can be helpful in communicating to the members the purpose of the church. They can be used to clarify and illustrate the statement of purpose, and to help the members understand the direction the parish is taking, the progress it is making, and also what remains to be accomplished if the performance is to match the purpose.

For example, the proposal to initiate a Thursday evening worship service for the benefit of persons who are out of town or at work on Sunday can be explained simply in those terms. Or it can be placed within the context of the statement of purpose which defined one purpose of the local church as providing the opportunity for corporate worship, and the goal as maximizing the opportunities for people to participate in corporate worship. If placed in this context, it may be easier for members to understand why a Thursday evening worship service was initiated and also why it is continued when the attendance is so low.

The poor quality of internal communication about the what and why of purpose and program is often a source of disruptive tension in a local church. If goals can be used to improve the quality of communication, an important fringe benefit may be a reduction in tension.

Another value of goals in the local church planning process is that goals can help enlarge the vision of the people. If old patterns are abandoned and new plans are developed based on new goals, there often is no limit to what may happen.

In one congregation this process was used to enlarge greatly the freedom of the local church. For decades the pattern of operation had been for the finance committee to prepare a budget for the following year, submit it to the church council for approval, and then go out to secure pledges to underwrite the budget. While it was never stated this explicitly, the process was based on three goals: (1) to keep the proposed budget as low as possible, (2) to secure enough pledged contributions to equal the proposed expenditures, and (3) to keep actual expenditures within the limits of the anticipated receipts. One result was that the proposed budget became a limiting factor in the operation of that parish. The budget, not the financial capability of the members, delineated the scope of the activity of that church.

After being forced to grapple with the question of the purpose of the church, the finance commission came up with a new method of operation based upon a set of four new goals. The first was to develop a good year-around program of Christian stewardship education. The second was to develop a level of giving related to the potential of the congregation rather than simply to cover the budget. This was a revolutionary move, for the proposed budget became a floor, rather than a ceiling, for giving in that church. In the past, during the every-member canvass, the visitor would say, "This is our budget for next year, and we would like for you to make a pledge to help us meet it." Now the every-member canvass is built, not around a column of figures, but around a threefold statement of purpose. When dollars are mentioned, they are mentioned in terms of the *minimum* amount necessary to enable the parish to fulfill its purpose. The emphasis is on the need to provide more than the minimum for each element in the church's program.

In communicating this to the members the third goal is explained. The third goal of this finance committee was to provide the maximum degree possible of freedom to the parish as it set about fulfilling its purpose. As the members looked back, they could see that budget restrictions frequently had blocked proposals for creative new program ideas. "There is no money in the budget for this; therefore we might as well forget about it," was the sentence often used to terminate the discussion when new programs were proposed. As they considered their role within the context of the purpose of the church, the members of this finance committee saw their old standard operating procedure as a blighting element in the parish.

Previously they had added up the various items in the proposed budget, and this sum became the target figure in their thinking and thus became the ceiling on giving and on expenditures for the entire parish. Now they began their financial planning by estimating the giving potential of the congregation. This new and higher figure became the target figure in their financial planning. The next question was to decide how the anticipated receipts should be allocated for the coming year.

Here the fourth new goal came into the picture. In previous years they had always accepted the denominational request as the "right" amount to put in the budget for benevolences. This figure became both the floor and the ceiling on their benevolence giving. Now as they sought to develop a balanced proposal for expenditures, they did this within the context of a balanced definition of purpose. Their short-term goal was to allocate one third of all receipts for benevolences, denominational apportionments, and other work outside their own parish. Their long-term goal was one dollar outside for each dollar spent within the parish.

For carrying out the every-member canvass the presentation to each member was built around three points: (1) the statement of purpose of the church, (2) the program that had been developed to enable the parish to fulfill its purpose, and (3) the goals the finance committee had used in its planning. The actual dollar figures of the proposed expenditures, which previously had been the central element in this presentation, were used only to describe in quantitative terms what was being done or being proposed. In three years, with this new emphasis on purpose and goals, this congregation with a stable membership more than doubled its receipts. Far more important, however, was the new sense of freedom the parish enjoyed as it went about the task of seeking to fulfill its purpose.

Goals are very useful in helping to clarify, communicate, and implement the statement of purpose. Perhaps even more significant is their value in helping churchmen look beyond today.

What Are the Consequences?

Unquestionably the most neglected step in the planning process is the element of consequences. This is true in city planning, in private organizations, and in churches. What will be the consequences of this proposal if we go ahead with it? Are there any consequences which we may not readily anticipate? If we decide to implement this proposal, how will that action affect our other plans? Questions such as these are important, but too seldom are they raised.

Goals can be very helpful in considering the consequences of a proposed course of action. First, goals force people to become more specific in their thinking, and the more specific and detailed the proposal, the easier it is to anticipate the consequences with some degree of accuracy. A natural and logical part of the goal formation process is the discussion of consequences.

Second, if the goals are clearly articulated, it is easier to evaluate the impact of the consequences and to plan in advance to counter any adverse consequences.

One of the most common illustrations of this in a local church is the decision to shift from one Sunday morning worship service to two. The immediate goal may be to increase attendance, to avoid the expenditure of money for a new worship facility, or to give people a greater choice. One consequence of such a decision will be to divide the congregation into two worshiping groups—one attending the early service, the other made up of those attending the second service.

If this consequence is foreseen, it is possible to structure other elements of the church program in a manner which will encourage people from the two groups to get to know one another.

The decision to move to two worship services brings into conflict two basic goals. One is to maximize the opportunities for fellowship. The other is to maximize the opportunities for corporate worship. When stated this way, it is easier for the decision makers to examine the consequences and to arrive at a rational decision.

A third value in the use of goals at this point is that this can offset some of the attractive but unclear phrasing that keeps clogging up the planning process and prevents appropriate consideration of the consequences. An excellent example of this is the recent emphasis in the church on "exploratory ministries." These are ventures in which the church adopts a new proposal without knowing where it may lead or what it may produce. Eventually someone begins to ask questions: What has been achieved? Should we continue to fund this venture? Is it a "success"? Since the venture was launched without objectives, goals, or any other criteria for evaluation, it is very difficult to answer these questions or to evaluate either the results or the consequences of this exploratory ministry. The usual response is something to the effect that after a period of time "we will meet and evaluate what we have learned."

Occasionally this can be helpful, but usually it is better to concentrate on "experimental" ventures where goals are articulated, objectives are specified, consequences are forecast, and a base is established for subsequent evaluation.

Basic General Goals

Any discussion of specific goals must be done within the context of the individual parish, its purpose, its resources, its people, and the needs of the community in which it is located. There are, however, three general goals which merit consideration in every parish as a part of its strategy development.

One of these relates to the need for a balanced statement of purpose as brought out in chapter 1. A basic goal in the local church should be a balanced program, one that gives appropriate emphasis to every element of purpose. Too often this goal of a balanced program is conceived of in terms of the clientele, or "something for everyone." While there is value in this point, the basic goal should be a program that is balanced in relation to purpose.

A second general goal with wide applicability also has been mentioned earlier. This is the goal of good communication, both within the congregation and out to the residents of the community. The effectiveness of the local church can be increased greatly if the people in the neighborhood know both *what* the church is seeking to do and *why*.

Good communication with the people outside the church is especially important when a parish undertakes a new program or when it decides to direct its ministry to a new direction. Occasionally this can be achieved by a single symbolic gesture. A Presbyterian congregation in the inner city in Little Rock called a new pastor with the avowed goal of shifting from a member-centered program to a neighborhood-oriented ministry. Shortly thereafter a prominent sign was placed on the front door of the church which told passersby that a new day was coming in the life and outreach of this parish. A few weeks later the new pastor and a few members gathered and painted the door Chinese red, and this event was filmed in color by a local television station and was shown on both of the evening newscasts. The new color symbolized the fact that "life is never going to be the same here again." Getting the television station to cover this event helped to communicate this change in attitude and outreach to both members and nonmembers. The bright red door has continued to communicate this change to people in the neighborhood.

A third general goal that can be adopted by every local

church is to secure the involvement of the maximum number of individuals in the policy-formulation and decision-making processes of the parish. This is important for several reasons. It is democratic. It utilizes the wisdom of a great many people. Participation is the best means available for a person to know what is happening and why. Widespread involvement of the maximum number of individuals minimizes the disruption produced by leadership changes as people die or move away. Experience also clearly demonstrates that the easiest method of securing financial support for any new proposal is to involve the maximum number of individuals in the development of the proposal.

A very creative illustration of the results of this goal of involvement can be found in the Church of Jesus Christ of Latter-Day Saints. When a Mormon congregation reaches a certain size, it is divided into two new congregations or "wards" with the result that the opportunities for service or involvement are doubled. Adult males are encouraged to enter the priesthood of the church, and the result is that there are six hundred thousand men serving in one of the two orders in a religious body with six thousand congregations. A very heavy stress is placed on personal involvement in the missionary program of the church, and the result is twelve thousand full-time missionaries. The church carries on an extensive welfare program for the needy and operates many farms where members contribute their labor to harvest the crops with the result that a Mormon lawyer, teacher, businessman, or housewife is personally and actively involved in this aspect of the life of his church, an act that has deeper meaning than simply dropping a check or a ten-dollar bill into an offering plate.

This concept of involvement is especially valuable in the assimilation of new members into the fellowship of the congregation. Frequently two or three years may pass before new members feel that they are accepted by the older members. A unique method of achieving this goal of early significant involvement of new members was developed by a thousand-member United Presbyterian church. In this church new adult members were received once a month and were asked to come prepared to spend the day on the Sunday they joined. After the conclusion of the Sunday morning worship service a brief reception was held to enable the older members to greet and welcome them. Then they were given a light lunch. During and immediately after lunch these new members were instructed in the techniques of visitation evangelism, and there was a quick review of the material they had studied in membership class about the purpose, mission, and program of their new church. They were asked to pair off, and each two new members went out to call on four or five of the persons who had visited the church during the past four Sundays. How better to learn the purpose and mission of your new church than to go out and call on persons who had visited it? How better to understand the evangelical concern of your new church than to go out calling as a representative from that church? How better to feel an essential part of this fellowship than to go out and invite others to join it?

It would be misleading, perhaps dangerous, to place such heavy stress on the value of goals in strategy development without also suggesting some of the pitfalls that lie in the path of the unwary.

Limitations and Dangers

The most common problem in the use of goals is that they may become ends in themselves rather than simply tools for implementing a purpose. The goal of raising enough money to meet the budget may smother the concept of stewardship. The goal of receiving fifty new members a year on profession of faith may overshadow the importance of assimilating these new members into the fellowship of the church or, even more important, of helping them come to the realization that Christ really is their Savior. Goals built only around service to the community can throw out of balance the original purpose statement of the church.

Unless care is exercised in the formulation *and the use of goals,* a perversion of purpose can result that can kill the parish or, what is even worse, leave it alive as an institution but dead as a Christian fellowship.

A second problem in the use of goals is that once adopted they tend to produce a degree of rigidity that can be undesirable at best and destructive at worse. As conditions change, priorities in the allocation of resources may have to change, and goals may have to be modified. Most people, however, find it difficult to change, and each additional element in the life of the parish that must be changed creates new problems and new tensions when change becomes necessary. It becomes easier to drift along in the old pattern than to change.

One of the reasons that it is difficult to change goals is that people tend to take great pride in perpetuating a condition that was the product of a hard-to-achieve goal. Perhaps the most common example of this is the congregation that went through years of struggle and sacrifice to become financially self-supporting. Eventually the day came when the parish did not have the resources necessary to carry out its mission in the neighborhood. Rather than seeking denominational assistance and thus abandoning the goal of being self-supporting, it ignored some of its responsibilities, cut back expenditures to keep them within the limits of the available resources, and continued to pride itself on being self-supporting. As time passed, the irrelevance of the church to its neighborhood became apparent to many, the resources were no longer adequate for even the curtailed ministry of the church, and the denomination was asked for help. Everyone involved knew that the older members were greatly embarrassed by this request for help, and perhaps some realized that the request had come too late. This was a request for help to survive, not for assistance in mission. Frequently this rigidity of attitude has turned what had been a commendable goal into a false god and has helped destroy another parish.

A third danger in an undue emphasis on the use of goals is that goals can produce destructive tensions in people. If the achievement of goals becomes an end in itself, it can have disastrous results. Instead of helping people become loving, neighbor-centered Christians, it turns them into object-oriented, frustrated individuals driven by a neurotic concern to achieve a relatively meaningless goal. Instead of helping them grow in grace and love, the pressure of irrelevant or unattainable goals puts them in the hospital with some psychosomatic illness. Instead of uniting a congregation around a common purpose, too much stress on goals can divide a congregation into several competing factions.

There are two sides to this point, however. The parish without a clearly defined purpose, the church without a sense of direction, or the congregation without an understanding of mission also can turn committed Christians into frustrated critics. Goals can be helpful in defining purpose, in giving direction, and in describing mission. Goals can be a means of translating purpose into performance, or they can be a source of frustration, anxiety, and tension. Perhaps the problem is not in goals, but rather in how they are used.

One of the most common limitations of clearly defined goals is that the floor often becomes the ceiling. This is a result of attempts to set specific goals which become ends in themselves. The clearest example of this in American Protestantism is the setting of goals by a denominational agency for the benevolence giving of local churches. A common pattern is for the denominational agency to apportion to each congregation a dollar amount for its "fair share." While careful efforts are made to see that these apportionments are related to resources, this cannot always be done. The usual result is that many members of the congregation regard the assigned quota as the most, as well as the least, that they are expected to contribute to this particular cause. Meeting the quota, rather than participation in joint mission and witness, becomes the ultimate end that controls the decision-making process.

Ideally, each congregation should determine for itself the

amount of money and the proportion of its receipts that it is going to allocate for work outside its own parish. This would be done as a part of the process of thinking through its purpose. The amount of money to be allocated for benevolences would not be an end in itself, but would be part of the implementation of a balanced statement of purpose.

There is much to commend this procedure over the common method of denominationally developed goals for benevolence giving. It has only one drawback. When a denominational agency apportions the amount a congregation is expected to contribute to denominational work, the result is that between 20 and 25 percent of the congregation's receipts are allocated for work outside the parish. When the congregation sets its own quota, the overall average falls between 10 and 20 percent!

The last, and unquestionably the most important, word of warning to be offered about the use of goals relates to the power of the Holy Spirit. The first two chapters of this book have been developed around the value of a systematic approach to the development of a parish strategy. The central theme of this entire book might be summarized in the words of a contemporary historian who wrote, "The man with a system, however inadequate it may ultimately turn out to be, has a vast advantage over a systemless rival, however brilliant." [1] While a systematic approach to problem solving is extremely valuable and goals are a fundamental element of any such systematic approach, neither the system itself nor

[1] From a section comparing Charles M. Beard with Carl Becker in Page Smith's *The Historian and History* (New York: Alfred A. Knopf, 1964), p. 112.

any of its components such as goals should ever be allowed to obstruct the work of the Holy Spirit. The one absolutely essential goal in the development of a strategy for a local church is that the members seek and be open to the guidance of the Holy Spirit.

3

How Can We Reach Out?

"Each year I feel that this church is becoming more and more irrelevant." With these challenging words, Jim Cole opened the discussion about the future of Trinity Church. Jim had spent all his life in the neighborhood served by Trinity Church. Now, in his late forties, he was the leading layman in the congregation and deeply concerned, not only about the institutional strength of his church but also about its mission and outreach among the people of the community.

"During the last fifteen years our membership total has dropped from about 525 to 364 members; church attendance is down to about 150 to 175 compared with a dozen years ago when we never had less than 200 at worship. Our Sunday school attendance is about half of what it used to be," continued Mr. Cole. "I know we pay all our bills and pay our apportionments for benevolences in full, but I feel we're becoming terribly ingrown and irrelevant. I am sure that an increasing percentage of our members are in their retirement years, and I know a great many have moved out of the neighborhood and drive back in to attend church. Anyone who looks around can see we are not reaching the adults moving into the neighborhood, although some of the kids are in the Sunday school. The Men's Club hasn't met for two years, we no longer have a young couples' club, and the adult attendance in Sunday school is only half what it used to be.

"The purpose of this gathering tonight," explained Mr. Cole to the dozen people gathered in his spacious living room, "is to talk about our church. I discussed this with the pastor, and he urged me to go ahead and call you together. He can't be here tonight—he has another meeting—but maybe that's just as well. Perhaps this way we can have a more open discussion."

"I'm glad you called us together," spoke up Frank Pearson, another longtime member. "I have the same feeling you have, that we're just sitting here going through the motions, and that we're not really doing anything or going anyplace. Our people just don't seem to have the enthusiasm they used to have. If we have a challenge, we meet it; but we certainly don't go out looking for new challenges."

"Now, let's not be too critical," interrupted Mrs. Williams. "This congregation is very loyal. When the Reverend Mr. White suddenly resigned, everyone pitched in until we got a new minister. When the furnace had to be replaced last November, we raised $5,100 in twelve days and had the cash on hand before the work was completed."

"That's just the point," responded Jim Cole. "When it comes to an internal crisis, we all rally around the flag, but what are we doing to reach out to the people in this neighborhood? In preparing for this meeting I did some homework. There are over ten thousand persons living within a radius of three quarters of a mile of our church. Less than 30 percent are Catholic. Out of the remaining seven thousand plus, not more than 3 or 4 percent identify themselves with our church. We are one of only three Protestant churches in the area. What are we doing to reach out to these people with the gospel of Jesus Christ? I'll tell you! Nothing!"

"Now don't get excited, Jim," said Bill Thomas in a soothing voice. "If these people wanted to go to church, they would. Every family in the area lives within a half mile of a church, and every one of these churches is open and eager to get new members. If the people moving in here want to go to church, they can. We could easily accommodate another fifty or one hundred every Sunday. Let's put the responsibility where it belongs. Let's not blame ourselves because most of the people living around here want to sleep on Sunday morning."

"And don't forget that our pastor calls in the neighborhood whenever he has a free afternoon or evening," chimed in Mrs. Johnson. "The people moving in know we're here, and they know they would be welcome if they came to our church. The real trouble is that people today just don't have the good old-fashioned values. They don't care about things such as church."

"Frankly, I don't believe in going out and dragging people into church," added Mr. Thomas as he sought to drive home his point. "I've been an active member of four different churches, and from what I have seen, I am convinced that the people who walk in and ask to join are the ones who turn out to be the good members. They're the ones who accept responsibility; they're the ones who carry their share of the financial load and attend regularly. Most of the ones you go out and beg to join disappear after six months, and they never do carry their share of the load. I think we're doing all right with the share of the market we have. Who wants this to become a six hundred- or eight hundred-member church?"

"I don't agree with you, Bill," spoke up Mrs. Pearson. "I think Jim Cole is absolutely right. We are becoming pretty irrelevant, and we are not doing anything in the way of evangelism or outreach. I believe as Christians we have an obligation to work a lot harder than we do at evangelism."

"Maybe the place to begin is to fix up our building so that it is a little more attractive," offered Frank Pearson. "Perhaps if we challenge our members by a specific program, we can overcome some of the lethargy. I know the church where my sister is a member really took on new life when they got into a building program. Our church certainly could stand some attention. Maybe we can kill two birds with one stone by starting a remodeling program. That will awaken our people and improve the appearance of our building at the same time."

"Let's be realistic about this," responded Bill Thomas. "First of all, our building doesn't need anything beyond what we provide for in the maintenance item in our budget. Second, our members aren't apathetic. They're just overworked. Every one of us belongs to so many organizations and has so many meetings to attend that we get tired. Today the competition for people's time is terrific, and the church is caught in this competition. Third, I admit things aren't what they used to be here at Trinity, but let's face it, the neighborhood is changing. The people moving in are different. The pastor was telling me last week about the reactions to calling on people in the neighborhood. The people know the church is here. They know they are welcome. Some of them are glad to send their kids to Sunday school, but they themselves are not interested. During the last couple of years, we have had three families from the neighborhood join the church. Two have already become completely inactive, and the third one is going to move to Georgia next month."

"I won't quarrel with your facts," said Frank Pearson, "but what do you propose we do? If we just sit here, we'll watch the membership at Trinity gradually dwindle away until someday the church will be forced to close."

"Now I'm not so sure of that," replied Bill Thomas. "We still have considerable strength, and I happen to know that at least four of our older members have remembered Trinity Church in their wills. While our endowment is less than $10,000 now, in another few years it will be over the $100,000 mark, and that interest will pay quite a few bills. If we could get more people to leave a bequest to the church, we could push this up to a half-million dollars, and then we wouldn't have to worry. These things run in cycles. Right now the people moving in either aren't interested in any church, or they're looking for a different type of church. Some day the pendulum will begin to swing the other way, and if we can just keep the church here, a different type of people will be moving in and this church will be full every Sunday."

What's ahead for Trinity Church? Will it fade out of existence as so many other churches have done? Or will people like Jim Cole be able to make this church relevant to the needs of the neighborhood?

It is apparent that the seeds of blight are present in this

church. Jim Cole sensed it. Any outsider listening in on the conversation in Jim Cole's living room would have perceived this. The congregation apparently is self-centered. It has lost both a sense of outreach and a receptivity to new people.

The answer to what is ahead for Trinity Church rests largely with the members. Obviously the congregation has the institutional strength necessary to be an effective instrument for the Lord. Will it use this strength and these resources effectively? Or will it slowly dissipate its strength until it is too weak to reach out into the neighborhood?

In discussing the future of Trinity three questions merit detailed examination.

First, what is the internal situation? Is there at least a committed, dedicated core of persons in the congregation who are concerned about the evangelical outreach of the church? Are they concerned about receiving new members simply to preserve the institution known as Trinity Church? Or are they interested in reaching unchurched individuals because these people also are the children of God and need to hear the good news of Jesus Christ? Are they concerned about the preservation of the institution or the redemption of individuals? Without this core of concerned and dedicated Christians the future of Trinity is dark indeed.

Are the members of the church open and receptive to newcomers? Or is this a closed church where the only new members who are assimiliated into the life of the fellowship are those who either are born into or marry into the congregation? Is this congregation really open to the Holy Spirit and willing to follow where led? Or is this actually a social club rather than a community of believers?

Going back to the simplified definition of purpose discussed in the first chapter, can we see that the blight of institutionalism has reached the point that this is a member-oriented church concerned only with the care of the congregation? Or is there also still present an understanding of the vital importance of outreach and mission? This question cannot be answered in general terms; the only useful answer is the answer given by the people at Trinity.

The second question grows out of history and experience. What is the experience of churches like Trinity? Is it possible for congregations that have become irrelevant to the neighborhood to become renewed, to reach out to the unchurched, to be a church in mission again? Or do they inevitably disappear?

History gives a mixed answer to these questions. Many parishes such as Trinity do eventually disappear. Some merge, others relocate, and many simply die through the process of dissolution. In a typical year an average of *at least eight Protestant congregations disappear every day* as a result of mergers and dissolutions. Like old soldiers, they just fade away.

On the other hand, many congregations go through a process that can best be described as renewal; they gain a new sense of mission and once again become relevant to the world and the neighborhood in which they are located. Experience suggests that perhaps one in four congregations in a situation such as that of Trinity will be renewed and again be a relevant and vital part of community life. Whether a parish such as Trinity will be in the one-in-four group or the three-out-of-four category will be determined by the power of the Holy Spirit and the response of the members.

The third, and most important, question to be considered here also grows out of history and experience. Is there any advice or guidance that would be helpful to churches seeking to reach out to the people moving into their neighborhood? Have we learned anything from experience that can be exploited by churchmen with the same frustrations articulated by Jim Cole? What can be done when a church finds itself out of touch with its community?

Many of the lessons that have been learned from experience are illustrated by what did happen at Trinity Church. While the members attending the meeting at Jim Cole's house could not agree on either the urgency of the problem or on a specific solution, they did agree to sign a petition Jim prepared asking the church council at Trinity to appoint a committee to study and report on the mission of the church for the next five years. A few suggested that this study should be directed at a ten- or twenty-year period rather than only five, but Jim Cole and Mrs. Pearson successfully argued that the next five years would be the critical period. If Trinity was going to undertake any important new efforts, it would have to move from its position of institutional strength. They perceived that it might take five years to get a ten-year program started, by then Trinity probably would be so weak that it would be concerned only with survival and have no resources available for service.

The chairman of the church council was very receptive to the proposal expressed in the petition, but he insisted that it would be unfair and unwise to appoint such a special committee until the church council was prepared to give direction by adopting a statement of purpose for the parish. After three months, seven special meetings of the church council, and considerable floundering, a five-point statement was prepared which emphasized, that (1) the gospel of Jesus Christ is a universal gospel, and the church must minister to *all* persons in the name of Christ; (2) Trinity would not relocate, but would remain at its present location; (3) the primary task of the church should be a neighborhood-oriented ministry; (4) evangelism and outreach must be given a greater emphasis; and (5) inasmuch as many of the present members do drive in to the church and there is a growing diversity among the neighborhood residents, the reconciling role of the church is a major challenge to Trinity.

After this relatively innocuous statement was approved by the church council, a committee of fifteen persons was appointed and given six weeks to investigate the needs and bring in a specific action program. There was some protest about the six-week deadline, but the chairman of the church council was adamant. He insisted that the biblical imperative is to act *now*; he argued that a prolonged study probably would not produce much more wisdom and might result in "paralysis of analysis."

Jim Cole, who was appointed chairman of the special study committee, did not participate in the debate on the deadline for the study. He had been so surprised and impressed with the willingness of the church council to come to grips with some very important questions that he felt it best to remain silent. While he believed six weeks was not enough time for an adequate study, he was reluctant to say or do anything to slow the momentum.

At this point it is worth examining what happened at Trinity. Five things stand out.

First, the meeting in Jim Cole's living room and the response of the church council demonstrated an awareness that perhaps Trinity was not as effective as it should be. The existence of a problem was acknowledged, with great reluctance by some but with openness and frankness by others.

Second, the leaders of the parish understood the need for a guiding statement of purpose and were willing to invest some time and energy in developing a relevant statement.

Third, and most important of all, there was a will to move, to come to grips with the call to the parish to become a more effective force in the neighborhood.

Fourth, while it is true that several of the people at Trinity saw the handwriting on the wall and were motivated primarily by a desire to perpetuate the institution, many others were more concerned with servanthood than with survival.

Finally, the leaders recognized that Trinity must be prepared to minister to diverse groups of people.

Once appointed, the study commission felt the pressure of the deadline and immediately divided itself into two subcommittees—one to study the church and the other to study the community. The executive secretary of the denominational board of missions was called in to meet once with each subcommittee and again with the total committee a week before the report was due to be presented to the church council.

On the advice of the denominational executive the subcommittee studying the church prepared a series of spot maps showing (1) place of residence of church members, (2) place of residence of persons attending two or more times during a five-Sunday period (Trinity is one of those churches in which church attendance is recorded every Sunday), (3) place of residence of regular attenders in the Sunday school, (4) place of residence of each leader in the parish, and (5) place of residence of each person who was confirmed during the previous three years. Next the list of the new members received during the past three years was analyzed, and the committee members interviewed each one, either in person or by telephone, to discover why that person had joined Trinity and to find out how active he was in the church now. Finally they made a quick analysis of the church budget in an attempt to see how the financial resources of the church were allocated among the three categories of congregational care, outreach and evangelism, and mission and witness.

The subcommittee studying the community turned to the reports of the United States Bureau of the Census to learn how many people lived in the neighborhood around the church, for an age breakdown of the population and for information about the education, income, occupations, and mobility of the residents. One person interviewed the principals of the two nearby elementary schools and the junior high school to learn what changes had been occurring in the past two or three years. Another interviewed the director of the YMCA to find out what he saw as the needs of the community. Six others each took a separate street and knocked at every fourth door. They immediately identified themselves as members from Trinity who were out to ask what the residents thought the church should be doing in the neighborhood.

Whenever they had the chance, they stayed long enough to listen, not only to hear what the neighbors had to say about the church, but also to hear what they had to say about themselves, their own problems, and the neighborhood in general.

What did these two subcommittees discover in this six-week period?

When they went over the results of their investigations and attempted to interpret the material with the help of the denominational executive, they came up with a number of conclusions.

From the work of studying the church, the subcommittee members found some fascinating geographical dimensions in the life of the parish. While nearly one third of the members, over one third of the regular church attenders, and approximately one half of the Sunday school attenders lived within one mile of the building, 88 percent of the persons identified as leaders lived beyond a mile of the church, and 56 percent of the leaders lived beyond two miles. "Colonial rule!" was the comment of one person when he looked at these comparisons.

"This is actually very easy to understand," explained Bill Thomas. "Our members who still live around the church are largely older persons who no longer are active leaders. The leaders in the parish are mostly middle-aged and younger persons who have moved out to new houses and bigger yards. The Sunday school reaches the kids of quite a few nonmembers who live in the neighborhood, and that's why that figure is so high."

"It's easier to understand than it is to accept," responded Jim Cole. "This verifies my concern. Trinity is irrelevant to this neighborhood. If we were a relevant church, we would be drawing more leaders from the community. Absentee land-lords can turn a good neighborhood into a slum, and absentee leaders can turn a relevant church into an irrelevant club!"

When they looked at the analysis of new members, they found themselves in for a greater shock. During the past three years Trinity had received a total of 51 new members: 37 by confirmation and 14 by transfer from other churches. According to the mission board representative, the average church the size of Trinity would have received about 100 new members in a three-year period: one half by transfer and one half by confirmation. The committee also found that while 29 of the 37 persons coming in on profession of faith had been teen-agers in the pastor's confirmation classes, only four of the 29 lived within a mile of the church, and 28 of the 29 were children of members. Of the other 8 persons who had joined by confirmation, 3 were persons who had married members of Trinity, and 5 were adults living in the neighborhood of the church. Only 1 of these 5 had attended worship at least once during the five-week period studied.

When they examined the list of 14 persons who had joined by transfer, they found 5 were in 2 families who had been members of the parish, had moved away, and had rejoined Trinity when they moved back to town. Three others had married members of Trinity and transferred their member-ship: 1 was the pastor's wife, and 3 were in a family in which the wife was the sister of Frank Pearson, and had joined Trinity at the urging of Frank and Mrs. Pearson. The other 2 were a couple who moved into the neighborhood, were called on by the pastor, and transferred their membership. During the same three years a total of 59 persons transferred out of Trinity. Twenty-three were removed by death, and 13 were dropped from the roll because of inactivity.

"That's a net loss of 44 in three years. At this rate in twenty years Trinity will be down to 75 members," announced one of the more pessimistic members of the committee.

"I'm not concerned about twenty years from now," interjected Jim Cole. "What disturbs me is that by the most generous interpretation we took in a grand total of 17 outsiders in three years, and 9 of those joined because of relatives, while 4 others apparently are now inactive. That means the net result of our evangelistic efforts for three years is 4 active members!"

"This shouldn't surprise you, Jim," said Mrs. Pearson. "When we examined the budget, we estimated that about 80 percent of it goes for congregational care and 20 percent for mission and witness, and that's money sent to the denomination and to the council of churches almost entirely. Unless we count part of the cost of hiring a minister, we can't find a nickel in the budget that we can say was allocated to evangelism and outreach here in this neighborhood."

"Contrast that with the fact that about 53 percent of our budget for this year is designated for the care and maintenance of our property, and you can begin to see where part of our problem is," added Jerry Nelson who had helped Mrs. Pearson analyze the budget. "I checked around with a half dozen other churches. The one closest to us in this respect spends 47 percent on their building, while the next

spends 34 percent, the next 26 percent, and the other three
are below 20 percent."

"Be careful now," warned Bill Thomas. "A good building
is an asset in attracting new members. I've heard that one of
the most frequent reasons people give when asked why they
joined a particular church is the attractiveness of the building. Isn't that so?" he asked, turning to the board of missions executive who was there to help interpret the findings
of the two subcommittees.

"Not exactly," was the response. "There have been many
studies made of this point, and it usually turns out that
only about 3 to 5 percent of the church members surveyed
point to the building as the reason for selecting the church
to which they belong."

"What are the reasons people give for picking a church?"
inquired Jerry Nelson.

"Far and away the most important factor is denominational
affiliation," replied the denominational official.[1] "Between
one third and one half of the people questioned say the
denominational label was the most important single factor in
their choice of a church. Lutherans and Episcopalians tend
to be at the high end of this range, while Presbyterians are
in the middle, and Methodists and members of the United
Church of Christ fall around the 30 to 35 percent figure.
Two thirds of all church members interviewed list the denomination as either the first or second most important consideration in their choice of a church. A national study made
by the United Church of Christ a few years ago revealed that

[1] For an elaboration of this point see Lyle E. Schaller, "Why People Join
Your Church," *The Lutheran,* November 23, 1966, pp. 18-21.

four out of ten members said the denominational label was a very important reason for joining their church—and that was in a denomination that we usually think of as being extremely ecumenical and placing very little emphasis on denominational loyalty.

"About 15 percent of all church members polled say their parents were the primary factor in their choice of a church, while another 15 percent point to the pastor as being the key factor, and nearly 15 percent more say it was a friend. These figures vary slightly among the various denominations, of course, but the important point is that four out of five church members say the most important single reason for joining their present church was either the denominational label or the influence of an individual. Among the remaining 20 percent, location was twice as important as program, and building was third. Don't count on the building doing your work for you in evangelism!"

"I'm surprised to hear people place that much importance on denominational affiliation," said Jim Cole; "but to me the important point in what you say is that nearly one half of the people say they joined their present church because of a person-to-person contact with some individual. It seems to me that this says something to us here at Trinity.

"In our attempt to study the community, we found the importance of this person-to-person contact," he continued. "When we went around and asked people what they thought this church should be doing, practically no one offered a suggestion. Oh, a few said we should be doing more for the kids, but no one had any specific ideas. In terms of getting ideas of what the people wanted the church to do, it was a waste of time, but there were two or three important dimensions to this survey. First of all, it forced a half dozen of us to go out and knock on some doors and listen. We didn't learn much about what the people thought about Trinity, largely, I suspect, because no one around here ever thinks about this church. However, we did learn something about the problems these people have, how they look at the world, and how they see the church. As near as I could tell, they see Trinity Church as a building, not as a servant congregation.

"Finally, we made a few friends. The six of us knocked on over four hundred doors in less than five weeks. About half of the time we managed to get invited in to sit down and talk for awhile. Together we found a total of seventeen homes where we not only were invited to come back, but where we *must* go back. These people need us, and we in the church must be responsive to their needs."

"Sounds like the six of you uncovered more prospects for membership in a little over a month than the entire church had been able to do in three years," offered Mrs. Johnson.

"At this point we're not looking for members; we're trying to discover what this committee should be recommending to the church council next week," interjected Jerry Nelson. "What else did you learn in your study of the neighborhood?"

"Those of us who went out calling compared notes last night with the rest of the members of our subcommittee," responded Jim Cole. We concluded that we have five alternatives for specialized new ministries in this area. One is to start a day nursery. There are lots of working mothers in this neighborhood, and a child care facility would be a real service. A second would be to start a program for "golden-agers"; there are over five hundred widowed women living in this neighborhood, and most of them are past sixty years of age. In addition there are many retired couples and a few widowed men.

"A third possibility," he continued, "would be to attempt to reach the teen-agers. The director of the YMCA seems to think this is the biggest unmet need. A fourth alternative would be to try to reach the young couples in their twenties and thirties. Both from our calling and from what we learned from the interviews with the school principals, we found that this is the age group in which the newcomers are concentrated. The fifth possibility would be to focus our energies on the people who have been left behind in the recent turnover of population in this neighborhood. We were amazed in our calling to learn that four out of five families have lived here for less than five years. The other 20 percent are the old-timers; many of them have been in the same house for twenty or thirty years. They tend to be elderly, lonely, somewhat apathetic, and pretty much overwhelmed by the changes that have taken place in the past few years. A majority of them are not really active in any church, although nearly all claim church membership somewhere."

"Sounds as if you have identified five target groups," commented the denominational executive. "Now the question is this: Which one do you want to give the number one priority?"

"Perhaps we could try all five to begin with, see where we

get the best response, and then concentrate there," commented Bill Thomas.

"It might be wiser to examine your resources, take a look at what the other churches and institutions in the area are doing, see where your resources come closest to matching an unmet need, and then concentrate on that one area of outreach," suggested the denominational executive.

This was what the group decided to do, and the following week the members recommended to the church council at Trinity that the church should develop a program to reach out to the young married couples living around the church.

Some objections were raised, both in the study committee and in the church council, to this recommendation. It was argued that the record demonstrated very conclusively that these people were not interested in the church, and those that were preferred a different kind of church.

Jim Cole defended the recommendation before the church council, and he offered several reasons why Trinity should concentrate on reaching this age group. He noted that this was the largest population group in the area and also included a large proportion of unchurched families. He pointed out that these were families and that Trinity was a family-oriented church with a program directed toward the entire family. The physical facilities at Trinity had been built for a family-type program. He emphasized that the location of the building meant that most of these families could walk to church and that therefore the problem of limited parking would be minimized. He referred to the seventeen families he and his five fellow visitors had encountered who needed the ministry of Trinity Church *and* who were interested in becoming better acquainted with the people from Trinity.

His most important comments, however, were directed to the people at Trinity when he explained what this recommendation would mean to the members. "We discovered that there are a great many needs in this neighborhood, but most of them are beyond our capability," he said. "We have only three assets. We have the message of Jesus Christ. We have a congregation of a few hundred members who believe that message. We have an adequate building in a very good location.

"On the other hand, we have many liabilities," he continued. "We have a poor record on evangelism. We have not been able to assimilate strangers into the life of our fellowship. We have been almost completely concerned with ourselves, and we have ignored the neighborhood and the people moving into this neighborhood. We have the reputation of being a cold and unfriendly church. We have ignored the people around us, and so they have ignored us."

"You sound pretty idealistic, Jim," commented one member of the church council. "What makes you think these people around here are going to change and start coming to our church all of a sudden? You completely overlook the fact that the people moving into this neighborhood are different. They have different values, and they have a different attitude toward the church than we do. Until they change their attitudes and their scale of values, there is no reason to expect they will be interested in our church."

"You've put your finger on the heart of the problem," responded Jim Cole. "There are differences. But are these people different from us, or are we different from them? Maybe *we* need to change! From our study of this situation and our experiences in visiting in this neighborhood I have become convinced that we can reach the newcomers living here if we're willing to make some changes in ourselves.

"First of all, we have to be willing to go out and call on people and get acquainted with them. I was impressed to learn that nearly one half of the people who join a church point back to a person-to-person contact as the primary reason for picking that church. We need to increase greatly our person-to-person contacts with the people in this neighborhood.

"Next, we have to open up and be more receptive to newcomers. We are going to have to learn how to assimilate new members. This includes trusting them to hold offices of responsibility. The day when you had to be a member here for five years before you could be trusted with a leadership position is past. This also means some of us may have to retire to the sidelines and make room for new leadership.

"Third, and this may be the most difficult of all for many of us, we're going to have to begin to realize that *we* may have to change. We must stop thinking that everyone has to become like us before they can come into our church.

"Finally, we are all going to have to work at this. Everyone in the congregation must become an evangelist, or we can't succeed. Some of us will have to get out and become acquainted and make friends with the people living around the church. Others will have different responsibilities, but we must all work at reaching and welcoming new people."

In reviewing what happened at Trinity several instructive

lessons stand out. The members began with a study of purpose. They successfully avoided the trap of diverting too much time and energy into study and preparation, thus leaving too little for implementation. Instead of making the common mistake of allocating their resources to remodeling the building or enlarging the parking lot or some other object-oriented effort, the leaders at Trinity wisely chose to concentrate their resources on reaching people.

They also realistically attempted to evaluate their resources, the unmet needs of the community, and the resources required to meet these needs. They decided they lacked the resources to open a day nursery or to undertake an effective ministry to teen-agers. They concluded that the appropriate match between their resources and an area of need was an evangelistic thrust directed to the young married couples moving into the area. They also recognized that this would require commitment of all available resources if the goal was to be achieved. Too often parishes decide to undertake a new task, but fail to appraise realistically the cost of the venture. Figuratively speaking, they allocate fifty cents of resources to a ten-dollar task and then wonder why they do not succeed.

The leaders at Trinity also saw the need to recognize that they, not the people they were trying to reach, might be the ones who were "different." They realized that this might require them to make some changes in their attitudes and actions.

Most important of all, in their attempt to reach out to the newcomers in their neighborhood, the people of Trinity recognized the vital importance of person-to-person contacts. They saw and accepted the value of an intensive and systematic program of visitation evangelism. During the first year of this new evangelistic effort the members of Trinity completed a combined total of over eight thousand calls. By the end of that first year every active member at Trinity, regardless of where he lived, had become acquainted and good friends with at least one or two of the new families who had moved into the neighborhood around the church in recent years. The statistical results of this visiting were not particularly impressive at first, especially in terms of membership figures, but during those twelve months Trinity had reestablished contact with the people of neighborhood. To a couple of hundred families in that neighborhood the word Trinity had become more than just the name of a building; it now symbolized people and friendships.

With the help of the dynamic leadership of Jim Cole the members at Trinity did not make the common mistake of leaving the responsibility of evangelism to the pastor, or to the pastor and a small committee. Evangelism became the central concern of the entire congregation. This is something one seldom sees in a local church related to the larger mainline Protestant denominations. In most of the parishes in these denominations evangelism no longer is a concern of more than a small percentage of the members. When a congregation does take its evangelistic responsibilities seriously, however, and when it places a major emphasis on persons, results do follow. This can be seen by examining what has happened in parishes like Trinity—and there are many Trinitys—and by looking at the spectacular growth record of the Mormons and of several Holiness, Adventist, and Pentecostal groups. Visitation evangelism is still an effective means of communicating the good news of Jesus Christ, and it also opens new channels through which the power of the Holy Spirit may work.

Three other aspects of Trinity's experience will also be of interest to churchmen who are grappling with the question of how their church may reach out to newcomers in the neighborhood.

At Trinity Jim Cole, the pastor, and a couple of other members understood how difficult it is for most church members to call. Therefore they made sure that the first call or two made by each member was on a family or an individual who had expressed some interest in Trinity. Their first list of "prospects" was composed of the seventeen families Jim and his five fellow committee members had visited plus some names supplied by the pastor. As members volunteered to go out and call, they were given names from this list. Jim, the pastor, and a few other members worked hard to add names to the list. After each visitor had completed a couple of calls at which he had received a friendly reception and after he had had his self-confidence built up, he was encouraged to call door to door.

The specific goal in this program of calling door to door was for each caller to keep on calling until he had met an unchurched person or family to whom he could relate comfortably. (Some members went out individually, some as couples, and some as teams of two.) Each caller was then asked to keep calling on that same person or family until the relationship moved from acquaintanceship to friendship. Each member was asked to find and cultivate one or two new friends in the neighborhood from among the residents without any active church relationship. The entire evangelistic thrust of Trinity was built upon the foundation of these newly established person-to-person relationships.

A second very important dimension of the experience at Trinity was unexpected but very beneficial—what had happened to the members who went out calling and made new friends in the neighborhood. While this was more noticeable among the members, and especially some of the leaders, who lived a few miles from the church, it permeated the entire congregation. The members acquired a new understanding of what was happening in the neighborhood, a new sense of the mission of the church, and a new excitement over the possibilities that were open to Trinity Church. It is only a slight exaggeration to describe this as the conversion of a congregation, a conversion that brought new life, new vision, and a thrilling new view of the future.

Finally, Trinity relearned how to assimilate new members into the life of the fellowship of the church. This turned out to be much easier than Jim Cole had anticipated. The primary reason that it was comparatively easy for this old, closely knit congregation to absorb newcomers was that most of the new members came in as friends of the older members. Instead of being viewed as strangers, intruders, or recruits of the pastor, the new members were looked upon as close friends of the Pearsons, or the Coles, or the Thomases, or the Johnsons, or the Nelsons, or of other families. This not only made it easier for the new members to be accepted as members and eventually as leaders, but more important, this new attitude also facilitated the development in the congregation of a new sense of neighbor-centered concern. What had been a closed fellowship built largely upon a foundation of tradition, nostalgia, and institutionalism became an open, but closely knit, community of concerned Christians.

When a congregation makes a serious and sustained effort to reach the unchurched, this will produce significant changes in both the attitudes of the members and the program of the parish. Usually these changes, including the unexpected ones, bring renewed life, vigor, and enthusiasm into the congregation.

This issue is a DEAD HORSE

4

How Can We Cooperate?

COOPERATIVE MINISTRIES

"The seven of us have been meeting together every Tuesday morning for over a year now. We serve seven churches from five different denominations, all of them located within a single consolidated school district. Four of the five denominations are represented in the Consultation on Church Union. At first we thought we would just get together occasionally to get better acquainted. I think every one of us has found these sessions together to be extremely helpful. Some Tuesdays we spend the time on Bible study, sometimes we talk over the problems we face in carrying out our ministries in this community, and some mornings I guess we just get together to shoot the breeze." The speaker was a trim, poised forty-year-old minister named James Grant. He was in his tenth year as pastor of a six hundred-member United Church of Christ congregation. He was one of eight persons seated around a large table in a classroom of a new $185,000 church building located on the rural-urban fringe of a large metropolitan area. The eighth person was a staff member from the state council of churches who had been invited to meet with the group that morning.

"Six of these seven congregations have been in existence for several decades, and four are in relatively new buildings. Two others are planning to build new facilities. The seventh is a new Episcopal mission started two years ago, and they expect to build before long. This building where we are meeting was built three years ago when two small, rural Evangelical United Brethren congregations merged and relocated here," continued Jim Grant.

"During the past several weeks we have been talking about how our churches might cooperate more in this community. We seven ministers find this weekly get-together a very enriching experience, but as churches all we ever do together is to sponsor joint worship services on Thanksgiving and Good Friday. We wonder if there aren't some other more meaningful ways we could cooperate. We wonder if we couldn't do a better job through a closer relationship. Two of the churches are thinking about hiring additional staff. Perhaps this should be shared staff. Maybe each one of us should develop a specialty and share that skill. Jerry over here is a crackerjack in working with youth. Wayne has always had a great interest in Christian education. A couple of us have had specialized training in counseling. In the medical profession the general practitioner is fading out of the picture, and the specialist is taking over. Maybe there is a lesson for us pastors in that.

"We asked you to come to talk informally about the whole subject of interchurch cooperation," he continued as he looked at the guest from the state council. "You've had a lot of experience in this field. You've had the chance to study different ways churches do cooperate and to see what works and what doesn't work. Tell us what's ahead for us if we try to develop some means of closer cooperation among these seven churches."

"Hold it!" interrupted a young minister who served the other United Church of Christ congregation in the community. "Let's not deceive our guest here by telling him that all seven churches or all seven of us see alike on this. I like and need the fellowship and support I find in this group, and I'm very interested to see what direction this discussion will take this morning. But that doesn't mean I want to be a part of a cooperative ministry. I don't want to be a specialist; I want to be a general practitioner. I want to be free when I get up in the morning to do what the Lord and my conscience tell me I should be doing that day, not what some executive director of a larger parish has scheduled for me to do that day. All I want to be is a country pastor. I don't want to be an organization man in a grey-flannel suit."

"Just so our guest doesn't misunderstand our situation here," added the minister of the Disciples of Christ church, "let me add my big reservation. I don't want to start anything that will lead into many more meetings. I already have too many meetings on my calendar. Let me read you a quotation I ran into a few years ago, and you'll understand my attitude," he said as he reached into his pocket and pulled out a small notebook.

Men meet together for many reasons in the course of business. They need to instruct or persuade each other. They must agree on a course of action. They find thinking in public more productive or less painful than thinking in private. But there are at least as many reasons for meetings to transact no business. Meetings are held because men seek companionship or, at a minimum, wish to escape the tedium of solitary duties. They yearn for the prestige which accrues to the man who presides over meetings, and this leads them to convoke assemblages over which they can preside. Finally, there is the meeting which is called not because there is business to be done, but because it is necessary to create the impression that business is being done. Such meetings are more than a substitute for action. They are widely regarded as action.[1]

"There a maverick in every group," smiled Jim Grant. "We just happen to have two, and maybe that's one of the reasons why we almost always have perfect attendance in this group. Now that we have heard from these two independent souls, we would like to hear what you have to say."

"There is nothing I appreciate more than frankness," began the guest. "Let me be equally frank and say very clearly that there is a limit to how much help I can be to you. I can share with you some of the lessons from experience, and these two comments illustrate two of the lessons we have learned about cooperative ministries. The first is that many men do find the structure of a larger parish or a group ministry too restraining, and they are not able to function effectively except as completely free and independent operators. The second is that efforts to develop cooperative ministries do require additional meetings; and unless great care is taken in

[1] John Kenneth Galbraith, *The Great Crash* (Boston: Houghton Mifflin Company, 1961) p. 144.

planning these meetings, people simply stay away out of frustration or boredom, and the whole idea falls flat. These meetings can become a substitute for action.

"In your situation here I would like to offer three general observations and then open up the discussion for your comments," he continued. "First of all, I strongly suggest that you look into some of the literature that has been developed from experience. Nearly every national denominational headquarters has materials available on cooperative ministries. Get these. A few councils of churches and church planning agencies also have put out pamphlets and booklets on this subject. These are worth looking at. The best book on the subject has been written by a professor down at Perkins School of Theology in Dallas.[2] It is oriented toward rural situations but has a lot of wisdom on the philosophy, the objectives, and the pitfalls in cooperative ministries in general. Most of the stuff that has been written about cooperative ministries in urban situations is so romanticized that it is not too helpful.

"The second, and by far the most important comment I have to offer, is to suggest that you look very carefully at the matter of purpose and goals. Why is cooperation being proposed here? Frequently cooperative ministries are developed for the wrong reasons. Usually churches aren't interested in cooperation until they are faced with the threat of extinction. Too often survival, not service, is the reason for cooperating, and that is no more than a fourth best reason. As one of my friends once said about these situations, 'It's like looking for a creative rat on a sinking ship.' The most effective

[2] Marvin T. Judy, *The Cooperative Parish in Nonmetropolitan Areas* (Nashville: Abingdon Press, 1967).

examples of interchurch cooperation are those that are created from a position of strength, rather than from weakness or desperation.

"Another element of this is the matter of lay participation. One of the biggest hazards in developing a cooperative ministry is the failure to involve laymen. Most of these ventures originate with the clergy; they are created by the clergy and they are dominated by the clergy."

"I guess this morning is a good example of that," interrupted the young United Church of Christ "maverick." "Here we are, eight clergymen talking about interchurch cooperation in this school district, and there's not a layman in the room."

"Good point," responded the guest. "The other item I would like to bring up under this matter of purpose is to ask whether you are talking cooperation around the matter of parish-oriented functions such as Christian education or leadership training or counseling, or are you talking about cooperation on issues?"

"I'm not sure I see the distinction," interjected Jim Grant.

"Traditionally most forms of interchurch cooperation at the parish level have been concerned with parish-oriented needs. The larger parish and group ministry both fall into this category," responded the visitor. "More recently we have seen many new, creative, and effective ventures in interchurch cooperation that are focused on issues such as race relations, fair housing, school consolidation, the war on poverty, community organization, public welfare, urban renewal, community development, and chaplaincies. Unlike the typical activities carried on in a parish framework, where an individual church can do a good job on a unilateral basis, when you get into issues, you usually find that the only effective approach is a cooperative one. You need each other if you are going to achieve the goal."

Twelve Questions on Cooperation

"Finally, I think we should spend most of our time this morning talking about the hard questions that should be asked in every parish that is considering going into some form of cooperative ministry," continued the state council of churches' executive. For the next ninety minutes the group discussed a variety of problems and questions under the leadership of their guest. He pointed out that these questions and issues had emerged from the experiences of those who have participated in or studied cooperative ministries across the nation. Their discussion can be summarized in the form of a dozen major questions.

1. *How does the traditional training of ministers affect the functioning of cooperative ministries?*
One of the greatest barriers to the implementation of proposals for new cooperative ministries is that the pastors of some of the churches that should be involved are unwilling to share in such a venture.

This should not be regarded as a surprising fact because the entire process of selecting and training men for the ministry tends to attract the "lone wolf" type. The call to the ministry is a highly personal experience. The model that most future clergymen see during their formative years is usually an inner-directed, independent, self-reliant, self-generating, and self-contained person who is operating as an individual and not as a member of a team. Seminary training may offer some encouragement for a team approach, but nearly all pastoral appointments and calls are to churches where the pastor is expected to function alone. The characteristics of the pastor's responsibilities, as well as the selection, training, and apprenticeship process, tend to produce the type of individual who is most comfortable operating by himself rather than as a member of a team.

One result is that relatively few mature and experienced pastors are found in cooperative ministries. Another result is that members of a cooperative ministry tend to be youthful, inexperienced, outer-directed, and more of a dependent type personality. (The common exception to this pattern is the minister who is the "Director" or first among his peers in a cooperative ministry or the minister who holds a position in a very loose form of cooperation.) A third result is that with the passing of the years many pastors leave the cooperative ministry and move on to posts where they function as individuals rather than as members of a team.

2. *Can the method of assigning clergymen be altered so that ministerial changes do not have such a disruptive impact on a cooperative ministry?*

An examination of cooperative ministries that have dissolved suggests that the critical factor often was a change in pastors in one or more of the churches. The new pastors had less interest in the continuation of the cooperative ministry than did the men they replaced.

In most Protestant churches the pastor either is appointed by a denominational executive or is called by the congregation (often from a list of names supplied by a denominational executive). It has been suggested by several advocates of cooperative ministries that at least some of the power for calling or appointing pastors must be assigned to either the group ministry or the parish council. Unless this is done, they explain, the normal rate of ministerial turnover eventually will destroy the effectiveness of the cooperative venture.

Another facet of the same question concerns salaries. The pattern in the past has been that most of the churches participating in a cooperative ministry tend to be small congregations, and the salaries offered are comparatively low. This severely limits the number of ministers who are "available" for appointment or call to a cooperative ministry. Furthermore, since ministerial salaries tend to be higher for older and more experienced men, this makes it difficult to attract experienced and mature pastors to these vacancies.

Thus it appears that unless alterations can be made in the method of placing ministers and in the salaries offered by churches in cooperative ministries, many of the new ventures in interchurch cooperation will be shortlived.

3. *Should efforts be made to institutionalize the cooperative ministry in order to stabilize its character and increase its life expectancy, or should the emphasis be placed on maintaining a flexible, freewheeling operation with a maximum degree of freedom for innovation?*

One of the reasons for the disruptive impact of leadership changes on cooperative ministries is that these changes usually occur before the new ventures have developed the built-in forces for continuity that are a part of institutionalism. If the structure and operation do become institutionalized, it is easier to absorb the shock of leadership changes; but once this has occurred, innovation becomes more difficult, and the venture loses part of its receptivity to creativity. Which is the more important element in a cooperative ministry: flexibility or stability?

4. *Can the advantages of an interdenominational base be reconciled with the growing demand for "denominational accountability"?*

Nearly every person who has participated in or studied cooperative ministries favors developing these ventures across denominational lines. A few have contended that *every* church in the geographical area served by the cooperative ministry should be included. While the price that would have to be paid to secure the participation of *every* church probably is too high to justify the results, the benefits of wide-scale participation are obvious. Most of the advantages of the concept are enhanced by broad participation.

On the other hand, several denominations have recently developed policy guidelines which require a procedure for systematic accountability between the recipient of denominational funds and the denomination. This strengthens the tie between the congregation receiving denominational assistance and the denomination. It also may make it more difficult for that local church to participate in an interdenominational venture. Problems develop over such issues as budget control, the representative nature of the governing board, the denomi-

46534

national affiliation of pastors, administration of the sacraments, polity, priorities, and placement of ministries. All or most of these problems are avoided when all the participating churches are of the same denomination.

Frequently the issue boils down to a single question: Does the value of having the cooperative ministry include churches of several denominations offset the additional problems created by this inclusiveness? Too often the response has been to brush off the question as one of minor importance. Subsequent events have often demonstrated that this was a question of major importance.

5. Is it reasonable to expect that a cooperative ministry can successfully include both large, well-to-do suburban congregations and struggling inner city churches?

Thus far experience suggests that the answer is in the negative. In rural areas it has been possible to bring several small open country churches in with a large county seat congregation to form an effective larger parish. In these situations, however, the similarities are greater, and the differences are fewer than in the urban situation where there appears to be a very limited community of interest between the large, strong, middle-class suburban congregation and the small, struggling inner city congregation.

On the other hand, unless a means can be developed for effectively bringing both suburban and inner city churches together in a cooperative venture, this eliminates one of the major arguments for more widespread use of this concept.

6. Can both weak and strong congregations be linked together in a cooperative venture?

This is a different question than number five, and the answer is clearly in the affirmative. While many cooperative ministries have been composed of only small struggling congregations, this is not necessarily the only or the best way to organize. There have been many very effective cooperative ministries which included both weak and strong congregations. The United Church of Christ in Ohio, for example, has had very successful results when moving from a position of strength and developing cooperative ministries around one or more strong churches.

Experience does suggest, however, that it is much easier to include both strong and weak churches if both are located in the same geographical area. This can be done in many rural communities where all the churches are in the same trading area, but it leaves unsolved the problem of bringing suburban and inner city churches together in the same larger parish.

7. Is it possible to develop a cooperative ministry that includes substantial participation by laymen?

Here experience suggests that the answer is yes, it is possible; but it is neither easy nor common. A variety of explanations can be offered for this low level of participation by laymen in cooperative ministries. Among the most obvious are these five.

(a) The institutional ties to a congregation are tangible, visible, and firmly established. By contrast a relationship to a cooperative ministry tends to be ephemeral because it is less tangible and visible. Institutional traditions and pressures tend to make it difficult for a layman to relate to any ecclesiastical organization other than his local church; and

when he is so involved, it is within the denominational structure.

(b) Sociologically it is very difficult to establish and sus-
tain horizontal relationships; vertical relationships are much
easier to develop. Therefore it is only natural to expect that
laymen will have difficulty in relating to another church
organization outside their own congregation. For those who
are open to such an additional relationship, it is only natural
that they tend to relate to other levels of the denominational
structure (vertical relationships) rather than to an area cooperative ministry (horizontal relationships).

(c) The overwhelming tendency is for cooperative ministries to be initiated by pastors and denominational executives.
Persons who are not involved in initiating and developing a
proposal are often apathetic during the implementation stage.
The common result has been that laymen have shown comparatively little interest in participating in the actual operation
of the cooperative ministry.

(d) Frequently authority patterns are confused in the cooperative ministry. This is in contrast to the typical parish
where polity, tradition, and custom have established authority
patterns that are comparatively clear. Duke Professor Daniel
Schores points out that in many of the group ministries he
studied the authority for policy making and programming
is informally vested in the ministers. He found that many
laymen believed that if they wanted to present an idea to
the interchurch council, they would not go directly before the
council, nor would they go to another layman who was a
member of the council. They felt, rather, that they would
have to go through their pastor or the chief executive of the

council. In effect the layman appeared to feel they were too far removed from the decision-making center to have any direct influence or even free access to it.

(e) Apparently the general tendency has been to make only very limited use of the skills available for helping small groups function effectively. The failure to utilize these skills, combined with the points mentioned earlier, often has meant that the typical layman has been encouraged to participate in the life of his congregation, but comparable encouragement has not been forthcoming to encourage his participation in the cooperative ministry.

In this day of a renewed emphasis on the role of the laity this problem must be solved if the cooperative ministry is to become a widespread characteristic of American Protestantism.

8. *Can the cooperative ministry overcome the building problem that has plagued so many ventures of this kind?*

One of the most frequent obstacles to effective programming in many cooperative ministries is an excess of obsolete buildings.

There are four facets to this issue. First is the matter of maintenance. Many small (and some large) congregations allocate over 40 percent of their financial resources to keeping the doors of the building open (janitor, insurance, utilities, maintenance, debt service, etc.). When this figure goes over 40 percent, it usually means that there is a shortage of money left over for programming, evangelism, and outreach.

A second facet of this problem is the loyalty of members

to the building. Any proposal by the cooperative ministry which can be interpreted as a threat to the future of "our church"—meaning the church building—probably will be rejected. This severely limits the options for action.

A third aspect is the nature of the buildings owned by the participating congregations. Often they are obsolete in design, no longer functional in size and space allocations, and poorly located. This may be an insurmountable obstacle when new programs are proposed.

Finally, the existence of these buildings usually causes everyone to assume that any financial assistance from the denomination should be for *operating* purposes only. It is extremely difficult to argue for denominational assistance for *capital* purposes when the cooperative ministry "already has more buildings than it can heat, much less use to capacity." The model for an answer to this objection is highly visible in the actions of consolidated school districts which abandoned obsolete structures at inappropriate locations in favor of a new functional building at an appropriate location. Unfortunately, the current guilt complex of many Protestants over building has made it difficult to develop this parallel.

Until and unless the leaders in cooperative ministries are able and willing to face this problem, their efforts will be severely handicapped.

9. Is the cooperative ministry the best—or the only—framework that encourages the innovator?

One of the most persuasive arguments in favor of cooperative ministries is that they have encouraged innovation while the traditional parish structure has discouraged innovation.

It is difficult to establish whether this was once a valid point or not. It certainly is no longer true. Recent experiences clearly demonstrate that innovators can function effectively within the traditional parish structure. The critical factor in providing a receptive climate for innovation is not the type, but rather is the age of the organization. A new organization usually is more receptive to innovation than an old long-established one.

Thus the burden on the advocates of the cooperative ministry may be to demonstrate that it offers an especially fertile field for certain types of innovation. Until this question is resolved, the proponents of the cooperative ministry may have to rely on other arguments to secure support for their plans.

10. *Is it really cheaper to operate as part of a cooperative ministry than as a separate, autonomous congregation?*

The answer to this is yes—and no. Yes, there are many operating economies that can be achieved through a cooperative approach. But no, it is not necessarily "cheaper" since total expenditures usually rise as a result of new programming efforts.

11. *Is it necessary to have one person act as the director or executive secretary of the cooperative ministry?*

Experience here is on the side of an overwhelming affirmative answer. There are a few proponents of cooperative ministries who contend that a council or a group ministry can fulfill this role, but nearly all the cooperative ministries and most of the effective ventures that have been in existence for more than a few years have had the advantage of a clearly designated leader who functioned as the director. Frequently this is a full-time responsibility.

In this, as in most voluntary organizations, the selection of a leader and the delegation to him of the appropriate amount of authority hasten the pace of change.

This answer raises the question of size and unit costs. A cooperative ministry of three to five parishes may have difficulty in financing the cost of a full-time director, while this is much easier in the larger parish composed of twenty or more congregations. The general agreement on the need for a clearly designated leader suggests a trend toward larger cooperative ministries which include more churches.

12. *What is the purpose?*

This is really the first question that should be considered by persons proposing formation of a cooperative ministry. Is it an end or a means to an end? Is it to be oriented primarily to issues or to people? (Anyone answering "both" to this question is evading a basic issue and asking for trouble.)

Is this proposal a response to a crisis? Or is it an attempt to improve the outreach of the churches?

Is it to encourage "social get-togethers" of members or to reach the "unchurched"?

Is this only an attempt to buy time and to postpone a difficult decision, or is it a sincere effort to enable the congregation to respond in faithfulness and obedience to the call of the Lord?

Perhaps the most helpful advice that could be offered here would be to regard this as an experimental ministry rather than an exploratory venture. This means establishing some standards for measurement of results before launching forth. It means that objectives must be clearly stated and be accompanied by a willingness to measure progress in achieving these objectives. It means that the initiators must be open to the criticism which accompanies experimentation.

The group ministry and the larger parish both offer tremendous opportunities for improving the effectiveness of the local church. This potential is more likely to be achieved if the purpose is clearly stated and if lessons from previous similar experiences are carefully studied.

What's Our Next Step?

After an hour and a half of this kind of background discussion Jim Grant sought to steer the conversation back to his immediate concern by asking, "Before we get into the specifics of our situation here, I would like to go back to something you said earlier. You said one of the biggest hazards in developing a cooperative ministry is the common tendency to exclude laymen. This same point was emphasized in our discussion here. What other hazards or pitfalls should we be especially concerned about?"

"There are two I would lift up for special consideration," responded the visiting expert. "One is the tendency for these ventures to have a relatively short life expectancy. Studies have demonstrated that less than one half of the cooperative ministries that are actually organized, and this doesn't include the hundreds that are discussed but never created, are in existence five years later. Some observers contend that less than one tenth ever celebrate their fifth birthday. The exact figures depend on your definition of a cooperative ministry. The important point is that the output may be limited by the short life, and you want to make sure that the input in creating it is not excessive in terms of the anticipated output.

"The other point I would emphasize concerns the institutionalization of the venture, a point we discussed earlier. This raises a very hard question. Which is more desirable: the freedom and probable short life expectancy that go with a loosely organized effort or the stability and continuity that go with a more highly institutionalized structure? I think the answer to this depends on purpose. My guess would be that if you're focusing around issues, you may not need or even want a lot of formal structure. On the other hand, if you're interested in a parish-oriented cooperative ministry, you may want a more elaborate and formalized structure."

"From what you know about our situation, what would you advise us to do next if we want to get something going soon?" inquired the Evangelical United Brethren pastor.

"First of all, think of the range of possibilities," responded the guest. "At one extreme you might want to form a new corporation that would be a sort of holding company, own all property, pay all salaries, and function as one congregation with five or six or seven decentralized meeting places. At the other extreme is what is represented here, for in effect you seven men constitute a loosely structured group ministry. If you are not satisfied with this, you may want to explore something more inclusive or more highly structured."

"Be more specific," pressed the E.U.B. pastor. "What should be our next step?"

"Let me suggest two alternatives," hedged their guest. "On

the one hand, you might want to call together a couple of laymen from each church and ask them to discuss some of the issues that your ministers have been talking about during the past several weeks. See if these laymen sense a need here for a closer relationship among the churches.

"The second alternative is to create a situation that will bring your laymen together, give them a chance to get acquainted, to discuss mutual concerns, to see that other churches face the same questions they are confronted with, in their church. A common approach is for a group of churches to sponsor a weekend retreat jointly. Typically, these run from thirty to forty-eight hours from beginning to end. You might bring in a team from the Ecumenical Institute in Chicago to lead this. They do an excellent job in their forty-four-hour retreat on basic religious beliefs.

"You might bring in someone to lead a discussion on the implications of the Consultation on Church Union. You might bring in a couple of laymen who have had a happy experience in some form of cooperative ministry. Out of such a retreat may emerge a consensus on an unmet need here that can be best handled through a cooperative approach.

"Just be sure that the purpose of developing a cooperative ministry is in response to a real need. Don't build an elaborate structure just because you feel guilty that your churches are not cooperating more with one another. The need or purpose may be simply to strengthen the total program of the churches. It may be to provide a unified Christian witness in the community. It may be evangelism. It may be social action. It may be for better equipping the Christians in this community to go out and carry on their ministry in the world. It may be to provide the framework for a better utilization of the skills of both clergymen *and* laymen. Try to define the goals as clearly as you can, and then begin to think about the structure or organization that is needed to achieve these goals."

"You certainly don't use the hard-sell approach when it comes to interchurch cooperation," remarked the Disciples of Christ minister to the visitor.

"I try not to," responded the staff member from the state council of churches, "and I urge you to use a low-pressure approach in talking with your laymen. If the merits and values of a united witness are not clear enough to encourage Christians to cooperate with one another, then we had better spend more energy on studying the Bible and theology and not resort to arm-twisting. Interchurch cooperation should be in response to a call, not the result of coercion."

SHARED FACILITIES

"How much longer do you expect to be meeting in the Highland School?" asked Jack White of his friend George Andrews. Both clergymen are in their early thirties, and both are serving as organizing pastors of new congregations located in a rapidly growing suburban community. Jack White is in his second year with the new Calvary Lutheran Church while George Andrews is the pastor of the one-year-old Aldersgate Methodist Church.

"We haven't even begun to talk about building," replied

the Methodist pastor. "If we can't find an acceptable church site pretty soon, we're going to be in real trouble. The rate at which land is being developed in this town, I sometimes think we'll be in the school forever. We looked at a four-acre site yesterday. The owner wants $70,000 for it, but it's the only adequate site at a decent location that we have been able to find. If we pay $70,000 for land, we won't be able to build for at least five years."

"The reason I asked is that we have a seven-acre site our mission board bought four years ago," said Pastor White. "I've been thinking that perhaps we should get together. We don't need all those seven acres, and I don't see any reason why a Methodist church couldn't be next door to a Lutheran church. We could sell you half of our land, work out a joint driveway, build one large parking lot, perhaps even share some building facilities. It would save us both money, it would provide a joint witness to the community, and we could cooperate on certain programs such as Vacation Church School, youth work, maybe a joint recreation program and do a lot of things together."

"Am I glad to hear you say that! I've been thinking the same thing, but I was hesitant to bring up the subject," responded George Andrews with great enthusiasm. "I was afraid it would look like we Methodists were trying to take advantage of the Lutherans' foresight in acquiring land. We are not competitive denominations; yet since the Lutherans aren't in on the Constitution on Church Union, there is little chance of our merging. I can see a dozen advantages to this idea, and I can't see any disadvantages.

"Let me share with you what I've been thinking," continued the Methodist pastor. "I see a long building with a sanctuary at either end. I think eventually we each will need separate worship facilities. Perhaps even these should be separate buildings. We'll leave that to the architect, though. In the middle we would have a fellowship hall, classrooms, a suite of offices—this type of facility. We could share all these, and look at the money we could save! The immediate effect would be that each of our two congregations could have the use of more space a lot sooner than if we go ahead planning two completely separate sets of buildings on two separate and very expensive parcels of land."

"Not only this," added Pastor White with equal enthusiasm, "but we could share one full-time secretary, rather than each have a part-time secretary. That way there would be someone in the office all day in case anyone called. We could operate with only one mimeograph, one set of office equipment, and we could cover for each other on days off, vacations, and emergencies. For example, while you are on vacation the two congregations could meet together, or I could lead the worship service for your people, and you could do the same when I'm away. Our people could get to know each other better. Lutherans would have a clearer understanding of The Methodist Church and vice versa. There is no reason why we couldn't have joint Bible study groups, maybe even have joint church school classes for some age groups."

"It certainly would encourage interchurch cooperation," agreed George Andrews. "It also would be good stewardship in the use of scarce land and would take less land off the tax roll than if we had two separate plants. It would save our people money, or perhaps I should say it would make it possible for us to make better use of the Lord's money. I can see a hundred advantages to this kind of cooperation. Creative cooperation, that's what we should call it. Why don't we both broach this to our people as soon as we can?"

"Maybe we had better think this over a bit more," cautioned the Lutheran minister. "This is a rather radical idea, and our members are going to have a lot of questions. We should be prepared with the right answers."

"Maybe you're right," agreed his colleague. "It is important that we don't make any mistakes either in presenting this or in carrying it through. I'll have to check it out with my district superintendent, too. Maybe we should do a little research on this idea, see what experience other churches have had with this, and make sure we ask all the right questions. As I think about presenting this to my district superintendent and to our people, I want to make sure that we ask all the right questions and that we give careful consideration to each question. We better know what's ahead for us if we do decide to go in this direction."

What is ahead for Calvary and Aldersgate if the two congregations decide to share facilities? What are the "right" questions to be asked? Does experience offer any help in answering these questions?

Four Types of Experience

Protestants have had considerable experience in the sharing of facilities by two congregations. These experiences can be divided into four general categories. The first, and the least relevant here, is the European experience. In many parts of

Europe two or more religious organizations share the same building. Not infrequently one is a Protestant group while another is a Roman Catholic congregation. The circumstances behind these cooperative ventures are so different from the American context that it can be misleading to use these as guides. They can be instructive and interesting examples, but are not necessarily relevant patterns.

A second set of experiences can be found in the hundreds of cases in America where one congregation rents meeting space from another parish. In this landlord-tenant relationship the renter usually is a small "called-out" congregation with a distinctive characteristic about its composition. Most often it is a group which uses a language other than English for worship. It may be a Latvian Lutheran, a Hungarian Baptist, a Cuban Methodist, or a German Evangelical congregation. Typically the adults are individuals who were born in another country and emigrated to the United States after the close of World War II, with their church remaining their strongest tie with the "old country." Literally hundreds of these congregations have been organized in urban America during the past two decades, and while many have been able to acquire their own meeting place, most have to depend on rented quarters. While of entirely different origins, some of the scores of congregations composed of deaf persons fall into this same category. Frequently they are too small, or meet too infrequently, to justify a separate building, and they rent space from another congregation.

Two generalizations from the experiences of congregations in this category are instructive. First, like many other land-lord-tenant relationships, these arrangements frequently produce damaging tensions over rental charges, conflicts in scheduling, cost of repairs or alterations, and either extending or terminating the arrangements. Second, in a great many cases the renter congregation is not satisfied until it has its own separate and exclusive meeting place. The reasons for this are many and varied; they range from convenience to status and often are sufficiently compelling to terminate the original rental arrangement.

The third type of experience in shared facilities is two congregations' jointly owning, operating, and maintaining one church building. The most common example of this in the United States can be found in Pennsylvania where scores of such arrangements were developed in the nineteenth century and continued for decades. The typical arrangement included one Evangelical and Reformed congregation and one Lutheran Church in America parish. The two congregations usually operated as completely separate and autonomous bodies, but they shared the use and the costs of one building.

As the economic pressures which created these arrangements were reduced with the rise in personal incomes, many of these arrangements have been dissolved, often with the encouragement and assistance of denominational officials. One minister, who spent part of his career as a denominational executive helping to untangle these alliances, has repeatedly emphasized, "If the only consideration that brings two congregations together in a cooperative arrangement is the desire to save money or to share building facilities, they are better off to stay away from each other. Interchurch cooperation must be based on something more important than economy or building facilities if it is to be meaningful and effective!"

Another denominational official commenting on the experiences of parishes sharing facilities said, "If they don't have a better basis for cooperation than buildings, they should stay apart; if they do have other reasons for getting together, then maybe they should explore merger."

The fourth, and most recent, type of experience in shared church building facilities can be found in some of the new ecumenical ventures. Two of the most widely publicized are in Kansas City, Missouri, and in the "new town" of Columbia, Maryland. In the former, four groups—United Church of Christ, Episcopal, United Presbyterian, and Roman Catholic—are sharing one new building. In the latter a jointly owned religious facilities corporation has been established to construct, own, and maintain buildings which will be used jointly by several denominations. It is still too early to evaluate the results of these newest experiences in shared facilities.

Questions on Shared Facilities

Out of these four different types of experiences it is possible to develop a list of questions that should be asked by members of a parish considering the possibility of sharing physical facilities with another congregation. This list of questions is not exhaustive, nor is there any suggestion that the answers will be the same in different situations. The questions are not intended to encourage or to discourage cooperative arrangements—only to raise some of the issues that experience has shown to be relevant and important.

1. Which facilities will be shared? Is it planned to share all facilities including those for worship and Sunday school? Or is the proposal to share only those facilities which are not subject to the strains of peak-hour use such as the fellowship hall, chapel, parlor, or kitchen?

2. Who will hold title to the property? Will it be a "partnership"? Or will a special corporation owned and controlled by the separate congregations hold title to the property?

3. How will the architect be selected for designing new structures or additions? By each congregation voting separately? Or by a joint committee?

4. How will the capital costs be apportioned? By membership? By participation? Will representation on joint committees be apportioned on the same basis as the apportionment of capital costs?

5. How will operating costs be apportioned? By membership totals? How will differences in the definition of membership be recognized? Will participation be used as the basis for apportioning operating costs? By which forms of participation? If on the basis of attendance at Sunday morning worship and/or attendance at church school, will this have an effect on participation? Will a member feel he is "helping" his church by staying home and sending his offering in by mail? If membership or participation is used for apportioning costs, how will adjustments be made if one congregation grows more rapidly than the other? Will such a basis for apportioning costs have an effect on evangelism or on keeping

a "clean" membership roll? Is there a built-in requirement for reviewing the basis for apportioning operating costs at regular intervals?

6. Will the fact that the title to the building(s) does not rest with the congregation have any adverse effects on raising money for capital expenditures? Will this influence the financing of operating costs? Will this affect contributions of volunteer labor? Will this influence the giving of memorials?

7. What happens if one congregation is unable to pay its share of the debt-service charges or of the operating costs? Does the agreement provide a plan for reallocation of financial responsibilities as conditions change or as crises develop?

8. Will one congregation have a voice in the selection (or appointment) of the pastor of the other congregation? Is there any method of reducing or eliminating the tensions produced by incompatible pastors? If one congregation decides to increase the salary of its pastor, will this decision influence or be subject to review by the other congregation?

9. Will the close physical proximity of two congregations enhance or reduce the competitive attitude of one congregation toward the other? What will happen if one congregation grows far more rapidly than the other?

10. Does the agreement of cooperation call for periodic review, evaluation, and possible termination of the arrangement? Is there a formula for apportionment of assets and liabilities written into the agreement? If one congregation dissolves or disbands, who gets title to the assets—the other congregation or the denomination?

CONCLUDING COMMENTS

The subject of interchurch cooperation at the parish level is attracting the interest of a growing number of churchmen. This interest is being intensified by the increasing attention given to church union and the possible impact of church union on the organization, life, and witness of the parish church. In attempting to look ahead and to evaluate the nature and the impact of interchurch cooperation on the parish, four considerations appear to stand out.

1. While it is tempting to denounce the "blight of institutionalism" as an obstacle to interchurch cooperation, it is much more realistic to recognize the necessity of institutionalized forms of the church and to accept these as part of the real world. These institutions and institutionalized forms of the church offer both assets and liabilities to the cause of greater cooperation. The liabilities can be minimized by a realistic and careful recognition of their existence. Likewise the assets can be enhanced and exploited more effectively if they are examined carefully and if credit is given to their source. For example, a careful analysis of the situation usually will reveal that "denominationalism" is not merely a liability, as is frequently charged by proponents of greater interchurch cooperation; it is also a major asset and can be of great value in furthering cooperation. Actually, of course, denominationalism is but one aspect of the institutional expression of the church and is neither inherently good nor inherently bad.

2. During the first half of the twentieth century, interchurch cooperation was focused largely on institutional arrangements and on parish-oriented programs such as Chris-

tian education. It appears that in the last half of this century the primary focus has shifted to issues and issue-centered ministries. This may be the most fruitful area for interchurch cooperation and should be explored thoughtfully by churchmen seeking new opportunities for a cooperative Christian witness. It appears that it is easier to develop a high degree of interchurch cooperation on issues than it is in such areas as person-centered ministries or joint use of buildings.

3. While institutional forms and the nature of the area of cooperation do influence the type and degree of interchurch cooperation, the most important single consideration is the commitment and enthusiasm of the persons involved. Without commitment and enthusiasm little can be accomplished.

4. Unquestionably the most important new consideration influencing the degree, nature, and shape of interchurch cooperation in the last half of this century is the new ecumenical spirit that is sweeping through Christendom. This new spirit of ecumenicity is making possible new ventures in interchurch cooperation that were not even dreamed of during the first decade following the close of World War II.

5

Should We Build?

"Should we go into a building program?" That question faces almost every congregation in America sometime during its life. In some congregations the question is asked every few years. In others perhaps only once in a generation.

During the decade of the 1950's hundreds of congregations voted enthusiastically in favor of a proposed building program. The amount of money spent on the construction of religious buildings rose from $558 million in 1950 to $958 million in 1960.

In the early 1960's scores of churchmen publicly began to raise serious questions about the boom in church building. Is it all necessary? Is this the best use of the Lord's money? Can we justify the construction of air-conditioned sanctuaries with foam padded pews and $40,000 organs when people are starving to death? Would it be more appropriate for the churches to invest these dollars to help the poor, the oppressed, and the hungry? As these questions were being asked during the early 1960's, the amount of money spent on the construction of religious buildings dropped steadily and reached a low of $850 million in 1964. By 1965 a new surge of church building (plus a rise in construction costs) pushed the total construction expenditures up to over a billion dollars for that year.

There are many reasons why a congregation should move into a building program. Experience has demonstrated the necessity of buildings as tools for the implementation of program goals. This lesson has been learned from experience in the inner city, in suburbia, and in rural communities.[1] For the local church to accomplish its purposes, it needs adequate tools, and one of these is suitable physical facilities. Usually, but not always, this means a structure that will be owned and operated by the congregation.

There also are many reasons why some congregations should not go into a building program, and these merit serious consideration by *every* church that is asking the question: Should we build?

Occasionally a congregation decides to build or to remodel the existing plant, not because this is needed for the church to accomplish its mission, but because this is a comfortable method of evading the real challenge. It is easier to plan a building program than it is to undertake an effective neighborhood evangelism program, especially if it appears that the newcomers to the neighborhood "are different from us." Often it is easier to interest a group of parish leaders in a building proposal than it is to interest them in a serious examina-

---

[1] For a discussion of why the storefront is less satisfactory than an adequate building in the inner city see Lyle E. Schaller, *Planning for Protestantism in Urban America* (Nashville: Abingdon Press, 1965), pp. 167-71.

tion of the purpose and program of the church. Usually a proposal to build a new educational wing or to remodel the sanctuary will win more support and cause fewer internal problems than a proposal that the church publicly support a fair housing ordinance or a suggestion that the church become actively involved in helping the poor gain a stronger voice in the community decision-making process.

Is the proposed building program necessary for mission, or is it a substitute for mission? Is it necessary, or is it only a means of postponing or evading a confrontation with more fundamental issues facing this parish? Is the proposed building program consistent with the mission of this church, or will it produce a false sense of mission? When it is completed, will the members view the project as an end in itself, or only as a means to an end? These questions should be asked in every church where a building proposal is being considered. Is this project necessary, or is it really an object-oriented substitute for the more basic person-centered programs such as evangelism, religious education, and mission?

The congregation that is considering a building program also should be aware of the potential blighting effects a building can have on the local church. Too often the building becomes a dictator. It dictates how the financial resources will be allocated, how the best leadership in the church will be utilized, how the pastor will spend his time, how much money will be available for the program, and what the program of the church will be.[2]

Sometimes a building program exhausts the resources of the

[2] For a more extended discussion of these points see *Planning for Protestantism in Urban America*, pp. 26, 122-29.

congregation so that when it is completed, there are no resources left for evangelism and mission. Is this a possibility in your church? Can your church afford to allocate this quantity of resources (energy, time, money, etc.) to a building program at this time?

In a great many churches, however, an analysis of purpose, program, resources, and needs will reveal that the congregations should give very serious consideration to a proposed building program. When this is true, people begin to ask a variety of questions. What is involved in planning a building program? How can we plan a successful building program? What questions should we ask, and where do we find the answers? Are there any pitfalls that we should watch for and avoid? What's ahead for us if we vote to build?

Some of the answers to these questions can be found by examining what happened at St. Mark's Church when they began thinking about building.

AN EQUATION FOR ACTION

"How many square feet of Sunday school space do you think we should build?"asked the chairman of the building committee at St. Mark's Church. His question was addressed to the church building specialist who represented the national board of missions of the denomination and had been invited to meet with the committee.

The meeting had started at eight o'clock that evening, and twenty minutes later, after an opening word of prayer, a very brief review of enrollment and attendance figures, and a quick tour through the five-room church building, the committee was ready to begin discussing the amount of space they should build.

"Let me interrupt for just a minute," said a member of the committee who was also cashier in a local bank and chairman of the church's finance committee. He addressed the denominational executive, "You should know that in this 320-member congregation we have 140 pledging units, and our total receipts last year were $24,800. I figure we can raise $30,000 in a three-year building fund drive. If we borrow another $40,000 beyond the pledges, we will have $70,000. A contractor told me we can build for about $12 a square foot. This means we can build 6,000 square feet of Sunday school space. Do you agree?"

"Let's slow down a bit," responded the denominational official. "I arrived in town less than an hour ago, and you're already pressing me for a precise answer to a building problem. The only way I can possibly be of any help to you is if we go back and start at the beginning. I admire your enthusiasm and your eagerness to get on with the job, but we may be trying to move too fast here. You're asking me for the answer, and I don't even know what the question is. Let's talk about the problem first before we try to define the answer."

"Oh, come now," spoke up one member of the committee impatiently. "The problem is pretty obvious. We have eleven Sunday school classes with a combined enrollment of nearly two hundred. We have three classrooms; one meets in the furnace room, one in the choir loft, two in the basement of the parsonage, two in the pews, and the senior high class meets in the pastor's study. Our problem is that we need more room.

How many square feet do you think we can and should build?"

"You may be absolutely right," answered the denominational representative, "but in order for me to catch up with where you are in your thinking, let's try looking at this equation for a few minutes." As he spoke, he walked over to the blackboard and printed these words:

PURPOSE → PROGRAM → FACILITY

"Thus far this evening," he continued, "all we have done is talk about the facility, the 'tools' you need to carry out the job. If we go back to the beginning of this equation, we see that we must start out by talking purpose. What is the Lord calling this church to do and to be? What is your purpose? How does this church justify its existence at this location at this point in history? Let's talk about purpose for a few minutes. What is the purpose of this church? Who wants to take the first crack at this? Let's try and be specific though, and think in terms of the local church."

After a long awkward pause, statements of purpose began to be articulated by members of the committee and were written down:

PURPOSE
    Worship
    Christian education and nurture
    Evangelism and outreach
    Missions
    Pastoral care

"This is a healthy discussion," interrupted the visiting denominational executive as he finished writing the words "pastoral care" in response to the comment that one purpose of the local church was to provide a counseling ministry to the troubled and the despairing, "and perhaps we should continue it. You might want to talk about the importance of this church's simply being here for those who want it in time of trouble and need as a purpose. No one has mentioned the prophetic role of the church, and perhaps we should talk about that. We should also recognize that everything we have listed here as purpose is a purpose within the context of servanthood. You may want to think of your whole building program in terms of servanthood and try to plan so that whatever you build, it will directly enlarge your ability to respond as a faithful and obedient servant.

"Time is running out on us this evening, however," he continued, "and let's see what this list of purposes says to us about the second part of this equation. If we think of 'program' as a broad and inclusive word, what kind of program are we talking about that will enable us to carry out our purpose?"

"Obviously the Sunday school is a programmatic response to the purpose we called Christian education," said the chairman.

"I suppose having a pastor available with regular office hours would fit in with the purpose you have listed as pastoral care," commented a third member.

As the members called out ways in which each program could be developed to implement specific purposes of the church, these were listed on the blackboard under program and directly opposite the appropriate purpose.

"You have listed a number of program responses to the basic question of purpose," commented the denominational executive. "Now let's move on and see what kind of facility we need to carry out this program we have developed. Should we start with worship?"

Within a few minutes the committee members had pointed out that if the church was to fulfill its responsibilities for a worship program, it would need a place to meet, off-street parking, a worship leader, hymnals, music, a choir, an organ or piano, and a music director. As these were mentioned, they were listed under the word *facility* on the blackboard.

"I hope you don't mind being called a 'tool' or 'facility,'" the denominational executive remarked to the pastor who had been observing the proceedings without speaking, "but this illustrates the variety of needs we have, or at least think we have, in carrying out the program of the local church.

"Next we need to add two more words to this equation," he continued as he went over to the blackboard. After the word *facility*, he added the words *resources* and *priorities*.

"In your planning here you need to review your resources and measure your needs against these resources. This will help you decide which needs rate the highest on your priority list.

"When we talk about Christian education, we naturally begin by thinking about Sunday school, and this leads us into talking about space. Before long we begin to think we can fulfill the purpose we labeled Christian education and nurture simply by building more Sunday school rooms.

"If we think about this for more than a minute or two,

we'll see that Christian education includes more than Sunday school and that we need more than just a building to implement this program. We need teachers, teacher training programs, and many other tools to carry out this program.

"Now, if you people as a committee go through this entire process, beginning back here with *purpose* and moving through to *program* and on to the *facilities* needed to implement that program, you will have a good overall view of your needs. I have a hunch that if you do this, you'll have more than just Sunday school rooms listed opposite the purpose of Christian education and nurture.

"As we drove over here from the airport, your chairman told me that you have been having great difficulty in getting and keeping good Sunday school teachers. Is this because of the lack of adequate meeting places? Or is it because of lack of training and support that your teachers become discouraged and quit? It may be that what you really need over here," continued the visitor as he pointed to the word *facilities* on the blackboard, "is a half-time secretary to take part of the office load off your pastor so he can be free to train your teachers and help them as they prepare for their task. If you add another eight or ten classrooms, where will you find the teachers?

"This brings up another factor we should talk about here," he added. "If you triple or quadruple the number of Sunday school rooms, you may also have a substantial increase in church attendance. As I look at your worship facility, it appears to me that you can't seat more than 175 comfortably, and a few minutes ago someone said you now average 160 at worship."

"That's just the kind of problem we would like to have," exclaimed the pastor. "We can go to two worship services and accommodate all who will come!"

"That may be," responded the denominational executive, "but you must recognize in a growing area such as this that when you increase the facilities for one phase of the church's program, you may be putting a strain on another part. If you build a 6,000-square-foot Sunday school addition, this may tie you up with a mortgage that will take you a decade or more to pay off, give you more rooms than you can staff, and overload the rest of your facilities."

"Wait a minute," interjected the chairman. "Are you suggesting that we may build more classrooms than we can use?"

"Not necessarily," was the response. "I expect you can use 6,000 square feet of additional Sunday school space, although that's about nine or ten rooms, and you may not *need* that many additional classrooms. What I am asking, however, is whether you can build that much without throwing your whole program out of balance."

At this point one member of the committee who had been silent all evening spoke up. "If I understand what's been said here, there are several facets to this question. We need more Sunday school space. If our Sunday school attendance goes up, and we know it will if we provide more and better space, our church attendance may go up to the point that we will have to go to two services. If we build an eight- or ten-room Sunday school addition, we may be so strapped for money while we're paying off the mortgage that the rest of the program will suffer.

"It seems to me," he continued, "that if we are going to keep this whole thing in balance, we have to provide more space for Sunday school *and* more space for worship *and* more secretarial help for our pastor so he can fulfill his responsibilities in these other areas we have listed under *purpose.*

"Would it make more sense to build only three or four rooms, go to a double schedule so we would have two worship services and two sessions of church school every Sunday, *and* hire a half-time secretary?"

Before anyone could answer him, another member spoke up. "I've been sitting here thinking, and it seems to me as I look at this list of purposes that we're putting too much emphasis on the Sunday school. When I think about the basic purposes of the church, evangelism and missions should be right up there with worship as the primary purposes. When you ask how we are going to assign priorities, I believe we should spend more of our time, money, and energy on evangelism and missions."

"This meeting is starting to get out of hand," interjected the chairman. "I thought when we adjourned the last meeting of this committee that we were all in agreement that we needed more Sunday school rooms. The purpose of having this distinguished visitor here was to help us decide on how many square feet we should build. Instead of moving closer to a decision, we seem to be getting farther away from an answer. This talk about purpose, program, and facilities has just opened a Pandora's box for us. Let's get back to the subject which is how many square feet of Sunday school space we should build."

"Perhaps that's our problem, Mr. Chairman," spoke up the youngest member of the committee. "We want to talk about building, but we should be talking purpose."

"You have a very good point there," responded the visiting denominational executive. "If you can decide on the purpose and on the programs necessary to carry out your purpose, you'll be able to see very clearly what you need for facilities. Once you have defined your purposes and developed a program to help you implement your purposes, you will be able to see if you are neglecting one aspect or overemphasizing some other element of the total program. This done, you should be able to see what facilities you need to implement this program, and in the light of your resources you can then assign priorities."

This discussion at St. Mark's illustrates three points that churchmen charged with developing a building program should consider very carefully.

1. The building should be thought of as a "tool" of mission, and therefore it should be designed to help the congregation fulfill its purpose. Too often the design of the building determines, rather than reflects, the purpose and program of the congregation. The building should always be regarded as a servant and never as the master. Natural institutional pressures tend to reverse this relationship; the building becomes the master, and the congregation devotes its energies to serving the building rather than to serving God.

If the members at St. Mark's had gone ahead and built an eight- or ten-room Sunday school addition, this probably would have meant that for the next few years the members and their pastor would have concentrated their time and energies on recruiting and training teachers for the Sunday school. It may be that a large and strong Sunday school should be the strongest part of the entire operation at St. Mark's; however, that decision should be made, not by a building, but by the members as a response to their statement of purpose.

2. If the congregation (or the building planning committee) can first state the purposes or mission of its church and then formulate a program consistent with those purposes, this can provide a very useful guideline.

As the committee members at St. Mark's began systematically to focus their attention on purpose, rather than on highly visible needs, they began to develop a more balanced and consistent program for fulfilling their purpose. As they reconsidered the purpose, they began to see other, less visible, needs.

3. Once a comprehensive statement of the "tools" or "facilities" necessary for implementation of the program has been developed and after this has been evaluated against the available and potential resources of the congregation, it then becomes much easier to assign priorities.

At St. Mark's some members of the committee were ready to make construction of greatly needed Sunday school rooms the top priority need and to allocate all resources to this single item. This might have been a wise move. It might have been a mistake. Some of these resources may be needed for the fulfillment of other purposes, but this could not be determined until a comprehensive statement of purpose had been formulated and studied.

It is very easy to ask, "How many square feet of space

should we build?" It is very tempting to direct the building committee's attention to specific questions such as this. An effective plan for action, however, must begin at the beginning, and that is with a statement of purpose.

THE IMPORTANCE OF A MASTER PLAN

"As we look back over seventeen years and three building programs, the greatest single contribution our architect made was in insisting that we develop a long-range master plan before we let him proceed with the design of our first unit. Several people in our congregation resented the delay, and they objected even more to the extra cost, but this turned out to be one of our wisest investments." The speaker was the middle-aged pastor of the Westminster Presbyterian Church whom the building committee at St. Mark's had asked to meet with them.

After two meetings with a denominational executive who specialized in helping parishes plan building programs, the building committee at St. Mark's had moved on to the selection of an architect. Out of the five architects they interviewed, only one had strongly urged them to develop a master plan before proceeding. Two others said it was generally desirable, but did not press the issue, while the remaining two never brought up the subject. When asked about it, both of these two architects suggested that since the committee was proposing a rather simple addition to an existing building, an overall master plan probably was unnecessary.

At this point the chairman of the building committee happened to spend a weekend with his sister in another city. On Saturday he accompanied his sister and her husband to a football game, and on Sunday they attended worship at the Westminster Presbyterian Church. On the wall of the fellowship hall hung a framed and yellowing copy of the master plan developed by the architect for that congregation nearly two decades earlier. When the chairman asked the pastor about it, he received an enthusiastic endorsement of the value of such a long-range plan. Since the two churches were only forty miles apart, the minister from Westminster agreed to drive up some evening to meet with the building committee at St. Mark's.

On arriving, the Presbyterian clergyman said to the chairman, "I would like you to meet the man who was my roommate back at the seminary. He is spending a few days with us, and since he is now a church planner in Michigan, we thought he might be of help to your committee."

The chairman took his two guests into the room where the building committee was assembled, and after the Presbyterian minister expressed his strong support for preparing a master plan before building, the questions came thick and fast. What do you mean by a master plan? How did you know enough seventeen years ago to prepare a plan that would be relevant a decade later? Who prepared it? How often did you change it? Can you give us concrete examples of how this saved you money? Were you primarily interested in a master plan for use of your land or for your building?

"Let's take these one at a time," responded the visiting pastor who had been taking notes during the period following his opening statement.

"First of all," he said, "our master plan was a joint effort by our committee and our architect. We first began meeting in a school, and after we organized as a congregation, we set up two committees: one to seek a building site and one to plan the building. We were advised to secure an architect early in this process, and he helped us select a good four-acre site. Thanks to him we didn't buy our first choice. He insisted that we have test borings of the soil made, and these showed that we would have an expensive foundation problem if we bought that site.

"Next this architect urged us to make a twenty-year projection of our anticipated growth pattern. At the time this seemed to be an impossible assignment, but with the help of the city planners and our denominational consultant on new church development, we developed this projection. We projected 300 members in 1957 and actually had 413; we projected 650 members for 1962 and actually had 720; we projected 1,000 members for 1967, but actually we had only 940 at the end of that year. In other words our growth curve rose more sharply than we had expected during the first decade and then flattened out faster than we had anticipated. We had projected a membership of 1,500 by 1975, but now we believe we should and will level off at about 1,000 to 1,200.

"In our planning we decided that we needed a building which would serve three major purposes—worship, Christian education, and community service—plus several secondary purposes such as a visible symbol of our existence as a congregation, an office for the pastor, a meeting place for committees, etc. As you can see, several of these are overlapping purposes.

"The architect then urged us to think of what we wanted to end up with in a building and to place priorities on these things. Our people wanted to build a sanctuary first and perhaps a couple of classrooms. Many argued that worship was our primary purpose. Our architect pointed out to us that what we really meant was that we were placing our first emphasis on a good physical setting for worship, but that might not mean we should build the sanctuary first. He blocked out for us in rough terms several alternative plans for a building that would accommodate a fifteen hundred-member congregation.

"At that time our congregation included fewer than one hundred families, and we began to get pretty nervous about our projections of eventually having fifteen hundred members, so we began to press the architect for more flexibility.

"He agree with us and developed a core unit which included a fellowship hall with a chancel at one end that could be closed off from the rest of the room. This enabled us to have a good physical setting for worship, but it also left the room free to be used for Sunday school classes and for large meetings and group activities. A short wing off this contained two rest rooms, the furnace room, the pastor's office, and two classrooms. The whole thing was planned so we could add on whatever we needed whenever we wanted.

"The master plan allocated space on the lot for a permanent sanctuary seating 600. Later we decided to have two worship services permanently, so we actually built a sanctuary seating 420. Our architect advised building this last. He suggested that by waiting we would have a better idea of the appropriate size and pointed out that it is comparatively difficult to enlarge the sanctuary without changing the proportions and thus adversely affecting the appearance. Perhaps equally important was the fact that the sanctuary cost us $33 per square foot while the rest of our building cost us anywhere from $10 to $16 per square foot. In other words we decided to build the most expensive space last when we had the most members and the greatest financial resources.

"How did a master plan help us?

"Let me give you several examples. First of all, we built in four stages: the core unit, two separate additions for the church school, and finally the sanctuary. The master plan enabled each new building to tie into the old with a mimimum of construction problems. The contractor told us that by having a core unit that was designed for additions we probably saved $20,000 to $30,000.

"Second, we ended up with one building that is aesthetically pleasing. From the outside it looks like one building, not a series of unrelated blocks. From the inside the unity is at least as apparent. Several people have told us that we have about the clearest and most logical traffic circulation pattern they have ever seen in a large church. When a stranger walks in, everything is where he instinctively feels it should be. Many of our newer members have commented on how very easy it is to find one's way through the building.

"Also very important was the fact that we could move ahead with laying out the drives, the parking, a small playground and picnic area, and plan the landscaping without worrying about tearing up part of it during the next building program. Knowing this encouraged our members to do an outstanding job in landscaping the property.

"Fourth, the architect developed the building plan in such a way that we had a minimum of interference with our program during the subsequent three construction periods. We never had to endure several months of disrupted program while the building was all torn up.

"Finally, and perhaps most important of all, the master plan enabled our people to see the whole picture. They knew what the eventual goal was; they could see each construction period as a step toward an eventual complete plant. This was especially important in working with those people who wanted to build a permanent sanctuary first. They could see that their desires were not being ignored."

At this one of the committee members spoke up, "What you say is very interesting, and I can see the advisability of a master plan, but not having one might not be such a catastrophe. It seems to me that if you design a building in such a way that it can be enlarged, you've achieved the same goals. Some people here seem to think that if we don't spend six months and several hundred dollars on a master plan, we're headed for disaster. I don't see the danger."

"Let me try to respond to that, if I may," interrupted the other visitor. "Back in Michigan I have been working with several denominations as a church planner for nearly a decade. Let me give you a few examples of how the lack of a master plan has been costly, and in a couple of cases nearly disastrous.

"One congregation completely overlooked the possibility that they might want to enlarge their facilities in the future. They placed their new building on the middle of the lot. Later, when they wanted to expand, they discovered that after meeting the required side yard measurement they could add twelve feet on one side and fourteen on the other side. If they had placed the original building to one side of their property, they could have added twenty-six feet to the other side. Their failure to plan ahead meant that they had to buy a $35,000 building next door and tear it down to provide the required side yard.

"Another church attached a new educational wing directly to a ninety-year-old white frame church. Eventually, when they wanted to tear down the old frame building and build a new sanctuary, they found they didn't have enough room. A master plan would have anticipated this and enabled them to see the necessity of erecting the educational wing as a separate structure some distance from the old church.

"I could take you to a church where they received a $4,500 bequest for landscaping. Eight years later about three fourths of it was torn out when they built the second unit. The sons and daughters of the lady who left the money in her will for the landscaping were so angry that they left the church.

"I could give you a dozen other examples of how a carefully prepared master plan can save you some grief, but let me take a couple of minutes and speak about some of the other questions that have been raised here.

"One of you asked whether the master plan should be for the land or for the building only. It should be for both! What we are talking about is a comprehensive plan for your entire property—both land and buildings. The use of one affects the usefulness of the other. To be comprehensive the plan must include both land and buildings, *and* it must be geared to your purposes, to what you are trying to accomplish.

"Someone asked how anyone can know enough today to prepare a plan that will be relevant two or three decades in the future. Another person asked how often a master plan may be changed or amended. These questions are related and point to the same issue. Above all else, a master plan should be prepared to ensure the greatest possible flexibility. We don't know enough to predict the future in detail. All we can do is to plan in such a way that we try to meet the needs of today and tomorrow as we see them and at the same time place the fewest possible restrictions on the decision makers of the future. This is true in planning the use of the land, in designing the building, and in developing a financial program to pay for it.

"Let me give you two examples of this. Between the Civil War and the Great Depression thousands of Protestant churches were designed on what became known as the Akron Plan. This plan was designed for a more informal worship service in which the sermon was the central element. It originated in the day when the Sunday school was geared to reach large numbers of people and the uniform lesson plan was used. Everyone, regardless of age, studied the same lesson, and Sunday school began with all classes assembled together for opening exercises. After the opening exercises were concluded, the people went to their separate classes.

"Eventually new ideas on Christian education were developed. Graded teaching materials came into use. The opening exercises were dropped. The worship services became more formal, and liturgy became more important. The divided chancel became popular. Unfortunately, nearly all the Akron Plan churches were designed and constructed in such a way that they could not be adapted to accommodate these changes. The buildings usually are very difficult to remodel; structurally they are sound, and therefore a congregation is reluctant to raze and rebuild. The result is that we have literally thousands of congregations operating under the handicap of an inflexible and functionally obsolete building. Today we recognize the reality of change, and many new church buildings have a high degree of flexibility built into their design.

"A second example concerns financing. I am now working with a congregation that eight years ago completed a building that is now inadequate. Unfortunately they financed this with a twenty-year mortgage and geared all their financial planning to this twenty-year mortgage. This means that they will not be free to move into another building program for a decade or more. The people today would gladly swap some of their excess space in the sanctuary for a couple of additional classrooms, but of course this is not possible. The decision makers of eight years ago developed an inflexible plan that will tie the hands of successive generations of decision makers for twenty years. If eight years ago the people had planned and constructed a building that could be paid for in six to eight years, the membership today would be free to plan and build what they now need.

"The best advice I can offer is that before you consider the details of the design of your proposed addition, you should develop a comprehensive master plan that has a high degree of flexibility built into it."

"Mr. Chairman," interrupted one of the members of the building committee, "while we have these two very cooperative fellows here, why don't we see what other advice they might be able to give us."

"Well, if you want to take the time," responded the church planner, "I would be happy to discuss with you some of the fringe benefits that may accrue to you during a building program."

"Sounds interesting," said the chairman. "It's only nine o'clock, so let's take a ten-minute break for a cup of coffee and then hear what else our guests have to offer."

FRINGE BENEFITS OF A BUILDING PROGRAM

The members of the building committee at St. Mark's had paused for a ten-minute coffee break and now were gathered back in the church parlor to talk with the church planner who was their guest that evening.

"Perhaps the best way for me to begin to tell you about some of the fringe benefits that may be realized from a building program is to share with you a recent experience," began the visiting church planner.

"One evening a few months ago as I was driving home from a dinner meeting, I saw the lights on in a new church. The pastor is a good friend of mine, and I thought I would stop, say hello, and take a look at how the new building was coming along. So I stopped, walked in, and saw that this was a work night for members of the congregation. The first person I encountered was a very active man who appeared to be in his early sixties. He was helping to lay the floor tile in the fellowship hall. He told me that the pastor was out of town for two days at a denominational committee meeting. We talked for a few minutes, and I asked him how the building program was going.

" 'I've been a member of this church for over forty years, and this is the best thing that's happened to this congregation in that time,' was his response, and he went on to tell a little about the history of that local church.

"The new structure was to replace the old two-room frame building which had housed this congregation for over a half-century. Until recently this had been a 150-member rural parish. In 1959, however, the continued growth of the large city in the next county resulted in the subdivision of several farms near the church for housing developments. During the next five years nearly a thousand new homes were built, and dozens of families began attending this rural crossroads church.

"First, the congregation decided to seek a full-time pastor and to have two Sunday morning worship services. Before long they were forced by lack of space to go to three worship services and to build an eight-room church school wing. This soon proved to be inadequate, and they realized that they would have to move to a larger site and build a completely new plant.

"It was obvious that the only way they could meet their current needs, much less provide extra space for anticipated growth, was to build by stages and to do much of the work themselves. That evening when I had stopped by, there were about two dozen men present, and they were scattered about the building, each doing what he could do best.

" 'For five years we kept receiving new members, almost every Sunday, it seemed,' continued the man who had been helping install the floor tile. 'I began to be able to recognize some of those who came to the same service I attended, but I remembered the names of only a few. It seemed like we were becoming two congregations, the old-timers and the new-comers, and I have to admit that some of us old members sort of resented the way many of the new people seemed to want to take over. The older members tended to stick together, and although I think I got along with the new people better than some of those who had been members here all their lives, I doubt if there were a dozen of these new people I could call by name. Now,' he continued proudly as he looked around the room, 'I not only can tell you the name of every man working here tonight, but I can tell you his wife's name and something about his family and his job. Working together on this building has made one congregation out of two groups of people who didn't know each other a year ago. Sometimes I think this has been more valuable than the new building will be.'

"The comments of this person illustrate one of the fringe benefits that may accrue to the church involved in a building program," continued the visiting church planner. "The primary purpose of a building program is to produce a tool which will be useful to the congregation as it seeks to fulfill its function and purpose. It is true that every church building program involves the risk that the members will become so deeply involved in the construction of a new structure that the building becomes an end in itself rather than a means to an end. This risk is widely recognized and has produced a considerable volume of criticism about the 'edifice complex' of contemporary Protestantism. Few will argue that there is not a sound basis for much of this criticism.

"On the other side of the ledger, however, experience has demonstrated that churches involved in a building program frequently receive several unexpected fringe benefits which strengthen the parish and improve its ability to serve. All too often little attention is paid to these benefits. In the typical year the local churches in American Protestantism will spend about $500 million of their current receipts on buildings and nearly $400 million more to pay off the indebtedness incurred in earlier building programs. Protestants spend twice as much on buildings as they spend on pastors' salaries. Approximately thirty cents out of every dollar dropped in the offering plate in the average Protestant church goes for construction costs—either directly or indirectly through interest and payments. Protestants spend twice as much on local church building programs as they send away for work outside the local church through benevolence giving.

"The magnitude of these expenditures strongly suggest that good stewardship requires any congregation contemplating a building program to consider how it can maximize these fringe benefits. While it is true that most of these fringe benefits affect the institutional expression of the church, they also may have a favorable impact on the spiritual life of the individual members. With a little forethought and planning it often is possible for a congregation to strengthen many different dimensions of its life through a careful analysis of the dynamics of a building program. In doing this it is helpful to know what to look for, and this raises the question: What are the fringe benefits of a building program?"

Unity Replaces Division

"One of the most common fringe benefits was illustrated by the experience mentioned earlier. A building program often can be the means of uniting a divided congregation through a common effort. As the members work together, they become better acquainted, they feel a sense of cooperative accomplishment, and they have a new opportunity to share another's burdens.

"Whether the division resulted from the influx of newcomers who could not be assimilated as fast as they moved into the community, or from some obscure episode years earlier, does not seem to matter. The coldness, the bickering, and the petty rivalries which dominated the atmosphere are overshadowed by the challenge of the building program. The forces which once divided the congregation dwindle into insignificance beside this larger effort which requires widespread support.

"This unifying force will be strengthened if the total building program includes a major emphasis on the participation and involvement of a large proportion of the membership. This involvement may take many forms and can range from the studies of the building planning committee to actual volunteer work on the construction of the structure, from service in the building fund drive to the training of the volunteer staff that will be working in the new plant, from the activities of the planning committee which sparked the idea of building to the work of the group which offered to landscape the grounds when the building was finished. A good building program will provide every member of the congregation with the opportunity for meaningful participation."

At this point one of the members at St. Mark's interrupted to assure their guests that while St. Mark's might have many problems, it was *not* a divided congregation. This precipitated a short debate as a couple of men began to point out some of the differences that were sources of tension. The chairman hastened to get the meeting back on the track by asking, "Are there any other fringe benefits of a building program?"

A New Sense of Purpose

"Yes, indeed there are," responded the visitor from Michigan. "There are four others I would like to point out for your consideration this evening. Perhaps the most important is the sense of unity and common purpose that may grow out of the Bible study groups that often are an early part of the total program. In these the members are confronted with questions about the nature, the purpose, and the form of the church. As the members strive to gain a better understanding of the biblical nature of the church so that they can advise the architect on the design of their buildings, they also may acquire a more profound understanding of the church as the body of Christ. Against this backdrop the forces that divided the congregation fade into insignificance, and the people can understand what Paul meant when he spoke of the church as one body with many members and as one member suffers, all suffer together.

"Closely related is the opportunity that a building program provides for self-examination. If a congregation sees the building as a tool for mission, then it must first define its purposes and goals before it is able to know what kind of 'tool' to buy. Should a new structure be planned simply to house the existing program which is running out of space? Or would it be better to examine first the program, determine what is relevant and useful and discard the rest, design new means of service to meet new or neglected needs, *and only after this has been done to begin consideration of the shape and size of the building necessary for implementation of this ministry?*

"This is hard work, and many congregations decide they are in too much of a hurry to go through this period of self-examination. In omitting this step they run the risk of constructing an unnecessary building for an irrelevant activity, *and they reject one of the most important fringe benefits that can be a part of a good building program.*"

Leadership Recruitment and Training

"A third contribution that a well-planned building program often makes to the life of a parish is the recruitment, training, and involvement of new leaders. While few churchmen like to admit it, in most congregations the same core of people hold the most important leadership positions year after year. Adoption of a plan which requires a rotation in office may help, but what usually results is a game of musical chairs that is played at every annual election. The chairs may be occupied by different players, but very few new players get into the game.

"A building program often changes this. It usually produces several new leadership positions, and these are positions which everyone in the congregation recognizes as being important, perhaps even of crucial importance. This often brings forth new potential leaders from among the less active members of the congregation. Whenever new leaders are really needed in a church, they usually can be found. The building program forces this search for additional leadership. The need is clear, and the nature of the responsibility is defined more precisely than often is the case with other leadership positions. In addition, many men feel more confident about their ability to lead a financial drive or to serve on a building committee than they would about serving as a teacher in the church school or as chairman of a committee on worship or evangelism.

"Whether existing leaders move into new leadership positions, thus leaving vacant their old offices, or new people are brought into the new openings for leadership, the result is the same. The core of active leaders is enlarged. This means, of course, that new opportunities are created for leadership training and for helping these new leaders gain the experience, skill, and confidence which will enable them to shift into other positions when the time comes.

"As the leadership group grows in size, the general level of participation rises. Most building programs are accompanied by an increase in attendance at worship and in other activities of the parish. This in itself is a very significant benefit, especially if every opportunity is seized to make this participation meaningful to the individual."

Impact on Finances

"The one fringe benefit of a building program that is almost universal is the impact on the financial affairs of the parish. There are three dimensions to this, and each one is important.

"1. The building fund drive may be the means by which a congregation first discovers its giving potential. It is not at all unusual for the members of a church in which the giving averages $125 per year times the average attendance at worship to believe that they have reached the financial ceiling for their parish. Three years later, after a successful building program, these same people are surprised to discover that the giving level now averages out to $200 to $250 per average attender. Couple this with the increase in church attendance which often accompanies a building program, and it means that the total annual receipts may be twice what they were a few years earlier. The building program enabled the members to see that the giving potential was much higher than they had believed.

"2. A building program often forces a congregation to adopt a systematic and well-organized approach to its financial affairs. The quality of the record-keeping may be improved. An every-member canvass may be used for the first time. A carefully prepared educational program may be inaugurated which enables each member to see the scope and variety of the ministry of the parish. New channels of communication between the church as an organization and the members as individuals may be opened up and improved.

"Each one of these will contribute to raising the level of giving. Perhaps much more important, however, is the fact that the use of this systematic approach also will strengthen the relationship of the members, especially those who are relatively inactive, with the parish as a unit. This improvement in communication will reduce the chances for misunderstandings to arise, counter the drift toward a sense of alienation on the part of some people, and help many of the members to identify themselves as a part of an active and dynamic church.

"3. As mentioned earlier, the building program provides the congregation with the opportunity to discover the real giving potential of the church. Once this has been done and a new and higher level of giving has been reached (often with most of the increase devoted to paying for the new building), there comes the opportunity to reconsider the allocation of these resources. How much should be allocated to work in the local church? How much to work outside the parish? What percentage should be allocated to benevolences to support the work of the mission board of the denomination? Does this new level of giving mean that the church now can more easily pay its quota for benevolences? Or does this new level of giving mean that the church can go the second mile in its giving and contribute more than its quota to the work of the larger church? These are important questions, and the higher level of giving produced by the building fund campaign provides the opportunity for raising these and similar questions about the stewardship of the parish."

A New Sense of Self-confidence

"A final fringe benefit of the building program comes with the successful completion of the effort. When goals are fulfilled, schedules are met, dreams are turned into reality, and the members gain a sense of accomplishment and confidence which should strengthen many other dimensions of the life of the parish. Most congregations lack self-confidence; they underestimate their own resources, and they doubt their own ability. A well-planned building program that is successfully executed may give the members of the church a feeling of achievement, confidence in the power of the Spirit, and experience of working together that will enable them to undertake challenging new ventures in evangelism and other new ministries to the people of their neighborhood.

"Two words of caution must be added in concluding this description of the fringe benefits which may be derived from a church building program," continued the visiting planner.

"First, these are *fringe benefits*. They do not provide adequate reasons in themselves for embarking on a building program. Too often a member is heard to say, 'If we would just get a good building program going here, we could wipe out the petty bickering that divides this church.' Or someone else may say, 'The only way to put new life into this church is to get ourselves a mortgage, so let's build something.' Both of these statements have a grain of truth in them, and both imply a recognition of the fringe benefits that often accompany a building program. However these are not adequate reasons for spending the Lord's money on a building. The only reason for entering into a building program is to provide a physical facility which will improve the ability of the church to carry out its ministry. Any other motivation may increase the blight which so often afflicts the institutional expression of the church.

"Finally it should be noted that a building program, and the fringe benefits that may accompany it, are largely directed to the church as an institution. It is very easy for the members to become so deeply involved in the various aspects of this program that they neglect other dimensions of the total life of the parish such as evangelism, the spiritual nurture and growth of the members, the outreach to the community, and corporate worship.

"I hope I haven't sounded like I was trying to sell you on a building program," concluded the visitor, "but I think it is important that in our planning we take advantage of every favorable consequence of a building program."

PLANNING FOR WORSHIP

"Back in college I had a roommate who always waited until the last minute before he would begin writing his term papers. About the day before a paper was due he would say, 'Now is the time to stop thinking and to start writing.' This committee has reached that stage. During the past few months we have spent a lot of time getting a variety of opinions on many different phases of a building program. Now we have about reached the point where we should stop seeking outside advice and begin to do some planning in specific terms." With these words the chairman of the building committee at St. Mark's opened another evening's discussion.

"I am not sure we have covered every phase of the program," responded another member of the committee. "We have done very little about a financing program beyond talking about a campaign to raise $30,000 over a three-year period. I think this deserves more study."

"I would like to see us look at what is involved in planning for additional worship facilities," added another member of the committee. "I realize we aren't going to build a new sanctuary now, but it wouldn't hurt to begin thinking about it so we don't box ourselves in with what we do build now."

These two suggestions struck a responsive chord among the other members of the committee, and before the evening was over, the chairman had appointed two special subcommittees. The first was instructed to study the question of worship facilities and to be prepared to report by mid-February. The other was asked to study financing and to have its report ready in early March.

The weeks rolled by very rapidly, but on February 11 the chairman of the subcommittee on worship facilities mailed to all members of the general committee a report prepared by his group. It included recommendations on four different items and began with a discussion of a very common question. Excerpts from the report of this subcommittee will be of interest to churchmen planning a building program.

One Worship Service or Two?

Any congregation averaging more than 150 persons at Sunday morning worship usually is confronted with the question of whether to have one worship service on Sunday morning or shift to two services. This frequently becomes a pressing issue when plans are being made for a new building. It will become an important question here at St. Mark's.

Many people prefer a Sunday morning schedule that calls for only one worship service. This eliminates the traffic problems, both inside and outside the buildings, that usually accompany any effort to crowd two services into the morning. It allows greater flexibility in planning the time and length of the Sunday school period. It allows for a full, unhurried worship service. When necessary, time can be allotted for baptisms or for the reception of new members without omitting some other element of the worship service such as the anthem or the responsive reading. If a missionary or some other visitor who is not accustomed to the schedule comes in to deliver the sermon, no serious problem is created if he speaks ten minutes beyond his allotted time. When this happens in a church with two or three morning services, the entire schedule is disrupted.

Perhaps the most frequent argument offered in defense of having only one morning service is that two services tend to divide the members into two congregations—those who worship at the first hour, and those who attend the second service. By scheduling only one worship service, the members see each other frequently, and this helps strengthen a sense of fellowship among the members.

As your subcommittee studied this question, we found very few parishes switching back to one service after having operated with two. There appeared to be two reasons for this. First of all, churches which have alternated between one and two services find that the combined attendance at two or three services is almost always larger than when only one is scheduled. A typical example appears to be St. Paul's on the other side of town, where they can seat 250 comfortably. For four years they alternated: one year they had only one service, the next two, the third year one, and last year they went back to two services. The years in which they had two services their combined attendance averaged 175 to 180 compared with about 160 when they had only one.

A second reason we found for two worship services was one of economy. As congregations grow, they find it cheaper to go to two services rather than to enlarge their worship facilities. We found only one parish where the leaders felt they could justify the expenditure necessary to enlarge the sanctuary so they could return to the practice of having one worship service. This was contrasted with three parishes where they either have or are planning to schedule three worship services on Sunday morning. In each case the members we talked with contended that they could not justify spending $25 to $50 a square foot for space that would be used only one hour per week.

The first recommendation of your subcommittee on worship is that St. Mark's schedule two worship services beginning the second Sunday in September. By doing this the opportunities for people to come together to worship God will be increased. Worship is one of the primary reasons for our existence as a church, and everything that can be done to encourage people to assemble to worship God should be done. We are convinced that changing to a schedule with two worship services will help us to fulfill this purpose.

Furthermore we suggest that consideration should be given to a Sunday schedule consisting of worship at 9 A.M. and 11:15 A.M. with a sixty-minute Sunday school session running from 10:05 to 11:05 A.M. With construction of the new educational wing we will be able to accommodate a full Sunday school for all ages during the Sunday school hour. We assume that a nursery and perhaps a kindergarten class will be operated during both worship services to care for small children. We trust the policy of the parish will be to encourage everyone from first grade on up to be in attendance at one of the two worship services. (While this is outside the authority of this subcommittee, in our visits to other churches we were very favorably impressed with the Christian education programs we found being carried on for both children and adults other than on Sunday morning. It might be wise for St. Mark's to consider shifting some of the "Sunday school" classes to 4 to 7 P.M. on Tuesday, Wednesday, or Thursday or to Saturday morning. We were surprised to discover several churches doing this with very satisfactory results.)

Equalizing Attendance

Next your subcommittee studied the pattern of church attendance in parishes with two worship services. We found that the usual pattern was for one to be about half as well attended as the other. A typical pattern in a church the size of St. Mark's is for the first service to average about 60 to 70 while the second will average about 130 or so.

The only exceptions we found to this pattern were in

parishes where a conscious effort was made to make both services equally attractive. In those churches where the second service was longer and where the chancel choir sang only at that service, the first service usually was attended by only half as many as were at the later service. By contrast, in several parishes we found that the two services were identical, the same choir was present in each, the sacrament of baptism was administered, new members were received at either service, and both services were of the same length. In these churches attendance often was nearly equally divided between the two. A couple of pastors noted that when one service appeared to begin to attract 55 or 60 percent of the people, they made an effort to make the other service more attractive. In one church the children's choir was the equalizer, and in another they shifted the larger of their two choirs to the less well-attended service. In a third, where nearly everyone seemed to prefer the second service which originally was at 10:30 A.M., they revised the schedule and moved the first service from 8:30 to 9:15 and the second service from 10:30 to 11:15. There appear to be many ways of equalizing attendance. Incidentally, we were surprised to discover that in two parishes the earlier service had the higher average attendance.

Our second recommendation, therefore, is that our goal should be to have two worship services, each with about the same average attendance. We do not believe that this goal will be achieved unless careful consideration is given to making the first service at least as attractive to people as is the second service. Perhaps the first service should be made *more* attractive than the second, and we urge that the official board be asked to study this matter.

If these two recommendations are adopted, we believe that it is reasonable to expect each service will average about 100 to 120 for a combined average attendance of 220. This would be a 37 percent increase over our present average of 160. Part of this predicted increase, of course, is a result of the growth in the size of the congregation.

The Eighty-percent Rule

One reason why we expect such a large increase in church attendance is that the combined attendance at two services usually exceeds the attendance at one. Another reason for our optimism is that we expect that the new educational wing will spark an increase in our Sunday school attendance, and our worship attendance should go up as our Sunday school attendance goes up. A third reason is our discovery of what is called the "eighty-percent rule."

This rule of thumb states that the *average* worship attendance in a parish seldom exceeds 80 percent of the physical capacity of the building. Thus if the physical capacity is 100, average attendance seldom will exceed 80.

In this church the physical capacity of our worship facility is 175, and we have been averaging 160, or about 91 percent. In effect we have been operating at over capacity, and we are told that this tends to reduce the frequency with which some people attend church. On many Sundays we have every pew filled and chairs in the aisles. This crowded condition tends to discourage some people who like to walk in and find an empty seat without being crowded. On checking the attendance figures we find that we do not have as many members who attend at least forty-six Sundays a year as do other congregations of our size which have more room. We are convinced that the eighty-percent rule does have a measure of validity and that by going to two services—and thus doubling our capacity—we can increase the frequency of attendance of many of the members of St. Mark's.

Our third recommendation, therefore, is that when we see that the combined attendance at two worship services is beginning to approach 80 percent of the physical capacity, we will plan to enlarge our capacity—either by building or by going to three worship services on Sunday morning. On the basis of the projections of our membership growth we anticipate that St. Mark's will reach this critical point in about six or seven years. Unless present trends change, we should expect to enlarge our capacity for worship no later than seven years from now.

What Should We Build Next?

Finally, this subcommittee studied the possibility of postponing the construction of additional church school rooms in favor of building a new sanctuary now.

Our recommendation is that St. Mark's proceed with plans to build eight classrooms now, rather than to consider either enlarging or replacing the present sanctuary. Two of the classrooms should be designed and furnished to serve as general meeting rooms with carpeting, sofas, and similar appropriate furnishings. There are three basic reasons for this recommendation.

1. By going to two worship services we can (a) accom-

modate our anticipated attendance for several more years, and (b) expect to experience an increase in average attendance as a fringe benefit of shifting to two services.

2. On the basis of unit costs (either square foot or hours of use) a worship facility is the most expensive part of the church plan to construct. We believe that St. Mark's should postpone this most expensive construction until later when we are in a better financial position.

3. Space for worship is extremely difficult to alter in size once it is constructed. Any alteration will affect the proportions of length, width, and height and will create problems of aesthetics. Therefore we believe that it would be best to delay the planning of any new worship facility until later when we have a firmer base on which to project our needs.

This report was discussed by the building committee at St. Mark's at their February meeting. The committee members unanimously concurred with all four of the recommendations and began to discuss the details of the plans for a new educational wing. Several members, however, were very apprehensive about whether the church could afford a $75,000 building. They anxiously awaited the report of the subcommittee on financing which was to be presented at the March meeting.

FINANCING THE BUILDING PROGRAM

"You have all received a copy of the one-page summary of recommendations prepared by the subcommittee on finances, and we will take as much time as you wish in discussing this report," said the chairman as he opened another meeting of the building committee at St. Mark's. "Perhaps the members of the subcommittee would like to lead us through their report and respond to our questions at the appropriate point."

"Basically our report is divided into two sections," began Mr. Whitney, who had chaired the work of this subcommittee. "The first part points out three important lessons we learned from studying the literature in the field and from talking with people who had led financial drives for churches around here. In the second part we have specific recommendations for St. Mark's.

"Everyone seemed to agree that it is easier to raise money for a building than for missions or staff or any other purpose. In fact, several claimed that the building fund drive could be so successful that it would jeopardize the current expense budget and benevolence giving. Therefore we feel that perhaps the most important lesson for us is that we make sure the giving level for missions and for current expenses is up where it should be before we begin a building fund drive. Currently we allocate 33 percent of our total receipts for work outside the parish. We urge that this percentage be raised to at least 33 percent before we begin a building fund drive. That would mean we would be giving for work of the larger church one dollar for every two dollars we spend locally.

"Likewise we see the need for a person who can do secretarial work and who also has the ability and willingness to help with the Christian education program and some of the general administrative responsibilities of running the church. At first, when we talked with the personnel committee, we talked about $1,800 a year for a half-time secretary. Then the personnel committee suggested it should be a full-time job. The more we talked, the more we felt the need was for an administrative assistant who would free our minister from routine but necessary tasks so he could spend more time on pastoral work. Finally we decided, after looking around, that we would have to pay about $6,000 a year to get the person we need. Obviously we cannot afford that now, or at least most of our members wouldn't think we could afford it, so we compromised on a salary of $5,600, and we are hoping we can find a person who will work three days a week at that rate. Thus the actual salary item would be $3,400 for a three-fifths-time person.

"If our membership increases as we expect it will, we should be able to make this a full-time position by the time we have five hundred or so members. We strongly recommend that this position be created and money appropriated in the budget for the salary before we start a building fund drive. If we don't do it now, we may not be able to for several years."

"Now aren't you getting a little outside the jurisdiction of your subcommittee on these specific recommendation?" interrupted Mr. Yost who was also chairman of the finance committee of the church. "It seems to me that these are matters that should be considered by the regular finance committee of the parish. As I recall, your subcommittee was simply asked to study how much money we could raise here at St. Mark's for a new building."

"You have an important point there," responded Mr. Whitney. "We started out simply to see if we could finance a new building; however, the more we studied the matter, the more convinced we became that the implications of a building fund drive go beyond the building itself. These two specific recommendations grow out of the first general lesson we learned about the implications of a capital funds drive. They are only recommendations, and we felt obligated to bring them to the attention of the other members. We would have been derelict in our duty if we had not done this. What the finance committee of the church and the parish will do about these recommendations is another matter.

"Before we get into any more discussion on this, let me simply state the other two lessons we learned. We believe both generalizations are relevant to our situation here at St. Mark's," continued Mr. Whitney. "In our second lesson we found that a parish normally begins to develop a building program around the problem of *needs,* but the actual scope of the proposed building often is determined not by needs, but rather by the financial *resources* of the parish. In other words the amount of money available often determines the final size and nature of the building.

"The third generalization we encountered is that churches tend to construct more buildings than they can staff and use. Repeatedly we ran into situations where a new building was only partially used because of the lack of program money."

"These are interesting observations," commented Mr. Davis who had been silent all evening, "but I fail to see what relevance they have to our situation. It has been pretty obvious to me from the time that we started meeting six months ago that here at St. Mark's we need more Sunday school rooms than we can possibly afford to build. I am sure that we will use every inch of space we can find the money to build."

"These two points help explain why we felt so strongly about raising our benevolence giving and hiring a second staff person before we get too far into the building program," replied Mr. Whitney. "If we are liable to build all we can afford, let's make sure that we *can afford* what we do build. In other words let's get ourselves committed to the appropriate level of expenditures for staff and for benevolence giving, and then use what margin we have left over for building. The common temptation is for a parish to commit itself to an overly ambitious building program and then not have the margin left for the other obligations. More specifically, if we create this second staff position *now,* then we are less likely to build more space than we can put to the optimum degree of use."

"I am sure we could continue this part of the discussion for the rest of the evening," interrupted the chairman of the building committee, "but in your report you have some specific recommendations for financing our building program, and I think we should hear these before time runs out."

Specific Recommendations

"Yes, we have three specific recommendations," responded Mr. Whitney. "The first one gets at the point raised earlier by Mr. Yost. We asked ourselves how much money we thought we could raise here at St. Mark's in a building fund drive.

"As you may recall, the subcommittee on worship last month suggested that we could expect to see our attendance at worship rise from an average of 160 to an average of 220 within a few years. We accepted the validity of their projections, and we did this without reservation because they appeared to be very realistic estimates.

"We found that the giving level in good parishes with a sense of mission and a building fund drive in progress often averages about $250 times the average attendance at worship. For St. Mark's that would mean we could expect annual receipts of $250 times 160 or $40,000, and that this will rise to $55,000 in a few years. Last year our total receipts were about $25,000, of which $5,250 was allocated to benevolences. *If* we add a part-time staff person as we suggested earlier and *if* we could allocate one third of our receipts to work outside the parish, we will have a total budget of about $36,000 for current expenses and benevolences. This would leave only $4,000 for a building fund.

"If it takes four years to reach the 220 level in attendance, we can expect our budget for local expenses and missions to be about $42,000, leaving $13,000 for the building fund.

"To make a long story short, we believe we can meet all our other obligations *and* raise about $20,000 from weekly and monthly gifts for a building fund during the next three calendar years. In addition we have good reason to believe that on our first building fund drive we can anticipate several large cash gifts which would total at least $10,000. Therefore our first recommendation is that we plan a three-year $30,000 capital funds drive."

"That's exactly the figure I suggested six months ago," interrupted Mr. Yost who was a cashier in a local bank as well as the chairman of the parish finance committee.

"Yes, it is," agreed Mr. Whitney, "but there is one difference between your earlier estimate and our recommendation. You suggested we could raise $30,000 for a building fund over and above a regular budget of $25,000. We are recommending an immediate increase of over $10,000 annually in the regular budget *and* a three-year $30,000 building fund program. In other words, over the next three years we believe this parish can raise about $35,000 *more* than you suggested last fall.

"Let me make it plain here that when we talk about a giving level of $250 a year times the average attendance at worship we are talking about a *good* level of giving. This is an achievable goal; many churches have reached it, and some have exceeded it. On the other hand some parishes average only $150 per average attender. For us here at St. Mark's it means a 60 percent increase in the level of giving."

"I see that," responded Mr. Yost unsmiling, "and how do you expect to accomplish this miracle? As I recall, my suggestion that we could raise $30,000 in three years was greeted with considerable skepticism. Now you are suggesting that we can raise over twice that much."

"You have an excellent point there," responded Mr. Whitney, "and that leads me into our second recommendation. We strongly urge that the parish make arrangements now to secure the help of a professional fund-raiser in the fall. We suggest that his help be used in *both* the every-member canvass for the regular budget *and* in planning and executing the capital funds drive. We do not believe the goals we have described can be attained without this outside assistance. The more we studied what has happened in other churches, the more convinced we are that we need this help. Whether this be one of the specialists in stewardship from our national denominational offices or a private consultant on fund-raising is a decision we believe should be made by the parish finance committee.

"Let me just say a word about our third recommendation since it ties in very closely with the first two," continued Mr. Whitney. "In our last recommendation we urge that serious consideration be given to holding the cost of any building down to an amount that can be paid for within a five-year period. More specifically, we believe that in our first three-year campaign we can raise $30,000. We also believe that a second campaign, running for only *two* years, would yield close to $30,000. In other words, let's hold the cost of our building program down to $60,000. This probably means building six rather than eight new classrooms.

"There are several reasons behind this recommendation. First of all, we saw very clearly that the easiest money to raise is for a building *under construction*. It is harder to raise money to pay off a mortgage, and the older the building, the harder it is. Therefore let's keep the term of the mortgage as short as possible.

"Second, it was pointed out to us a few weeks ago that it is highly desirable not to bind the hands of the future decision makers in the parish. Therefore let's not build more than we can pay off in five years. When that is paid for, let the people who are making the decisions at that date decide what to do next. If they want to build more Sunday school rooms at that time, let that be their decision. If it is *their* decision, they will have more interest in developing the program and in paying off the new indebtedness. Let's leave them the maximum degree of flexibility in their planning.

"Third, and this is a bit out of our field, but from everything we have heard and seen, we wonder just how much space for Christian education we really do need. The trend seems to be to take Christian education out of Sunday morning and put it in the program during the week. If we move in that direction, in five years we may have six, not twelve or fourteen classes on Sunday morning.

"Fourth, and perhaps most important, every member of our subcommittee agrees this six months of study and discussion has been extremely stimulating and rewarding. I expect most members of the general committee feel the same way. Therefore, if we limit the size of our building program to a $60,000 package now *and if* it turns out that in four or five years we do need more building, that need will provide the opportunity for another group of members from this parish to profit by a learning experience similar to ours. Frankly, I covet that opportunity for every member of this church."

"Thank you, Mr. Whitney," said the chairman, "for a very fine report. You have presented us with some very provocative recommendations and suggestions. I think your entire report illustrates your last point very clearly. We are all wiser and better informed as a result of this opportunity to have had joint study and free discussion."

While the problems you will encounter if your church moves into a building program may not be exactly the same as those discussed at St. Mark's, their experiences may help you see what's ahead for your church if you decide to build.

6

What Is Ahead for Old First Church?

"Last fall the congregation overwhelmingly rejected a proposal that we merge with St. Paul's Church on the north edge of town. Three years ago the members turned down, by a two to one vote, a proposal to relocate in a new residential area being developed on the far west side. That was something of a surprise for many of us since the proposed site would have been closer to the homes of nearly one half of our members. Shortly after that decision the board of missions went in and started a new mission there which now has over three hundred members, including about thirty families who formerly belonged to First Church.

"We've decided what we are *not* going to do. We're not going to merge, and we're not going to relocate, but we haven't decided anything affirmatively. What are we *going* to do? Just sit here and watch the years go by until we fade from the scene? There used to be seven churches in the central business district of this city. Today there are only three left. Three of the other four have relocated, and the fourth merged with a sister church. Is there any future for the downtown church? What's ahead for us if we stay here?" The speaker was the lay leader of the oldest church in the city. He also was serving as chairman of a special seven-man planning committee that had been appointed to study the future of old First Church. At its third meeting the committee had agreed to call in as a special consultant the church planner on the staff of the state council of churches. This Saturday afternoon was his first meeting with the committee.

Old First Church was at a critical point in its history. The sixty-year-old building was located a short block from the center of the downtown retail district. A modification of the old Akron Plan design, it was structurally sound, but functionally obsolete. The sanctuary had been remodeled, so that it now provided an adequate physical setting for worship, and a new three-story church school wing with a large fellowship hall had been added fifteen years earlier. Despite these improvements the building was expensive to maintain and operate, it presented a forbidding appearance to strangers, and it included a vast amount of unusable and unused space.

Since the turn of the century First Church had "mothered" four of the five other churches of its denomination in the city. It had also cooperated with the denominational board of missions in launching the two newest congregations— the one on the far west side of town and a new year-old mission in a suburban community to the south. For decades First Church had been the largest church of its denomination in the community, but now its eleven hundred members placed it second in size to St. Luke's on the east side.

"The immediate reason for our asking you to meet with

us," continued the lay leader as he addressed the visitor, "is that our senior minister has announced that he is retiring in six months. He has served as pastor of this church for twenty-three years, and we are grateful for his leadership. The time has come, however, when we must do some good, sound planning ourselves. We cannot depend on the ministers to do this for us. It is time for the laymen in this church to get together and do some serious thinking about the future of this church."

"So far all we have been able to do is come up with a lot of questions and very few answers," interjected Mr. Wallace who was president of the biggest department store in town. "What's the role of the downtown church in today's world? Everyone is moving out to the new residential districts on the periphery of the city. It used to be that the business and professional people moving into the community automatically joined one of the downtown churches. Now they buy a house several miles out and go to one of the new neighborhood churches. What's our future?"

"You've identified one of the changes that is confronting many downtown churches," responded the visiting church planner, "and this change illustrates some of the forces that are affecting churches such as this one. You said that formerly newcomers frequently joined one of the downtown churches when they moved into the community. This was true. The downtown church usually served as a kind of port of entry for newcomers to the city. This is still a function for some downtown churches, but today most people moving to a city seek out a church closer to where they live. Typically this is an outlying church in a residential district rather than the downtown church.

"This one change is not of fundamental importance in itself," continued the church planner, "but it symbolizes the forces that have affected the role of the downtown church. The most important single force has been the trend toward decentralization and suburbanization of the population, and the organization of new congregations out in the new residential areas. This same pressure for decentralization also can be seen in retail trade, industrial employment, recreation, entertainment, and other segments of the economy. The result is a decline in the comparative importance of the central business district as *the* focal point of the community. This affects the role of the downtown church. Just as the central part of the city is no longer the point of entry for the newcomer, so it is that many residents of the community rarely get into the downtown district. In many metropolitan areas thousands of residents never come near the central business district more than once or twice a year, if that often. One result is that in many larger cities the downtown church is disappearing from the scene. In general, the larger the city and the greater the extent of urbanization, the fewer the number of downtown 'First' type churches in proportion to the population. In Fort Wayne, Indiana, for example, in a city with a population of 175,000, there are about eight large downtown churches. In Miami, Florida, with nearly twice as many residents, there are only three mainline Protestant churches in the downtown area north of the river. In Cleveland, Ohio, with a population of 825,000, there are only two Protestant downtown churches.

"Closely related to this decentralization trend is another important change. In many of the emerging new cities, especially the newer suburban cities, there is no clearly defined geographical focal point for the community. There is no downtown. You can drive through the community without knowing when you entered and when you left it. There is no central business district. As a result we have many cities in the 25,000 to 100,000 population range without a downtown area and therefore without any 'downtown' churches. This does not mean, however, that there are not any large parishes in these communities that are comparable in many ways to the old First Church in the downtown area of the central city."

"That's very interesting," said Robert Jackson, an attorney who was also the youngest member on First Church's planning committee, "but what does that have to do with us?"

"Perhaps the most important point," was the response, "is that it helps us sharpen our definitions. We're beginning to see that there is a difference between a downtown church that carries on the ministries and programs one often associates with a downtown church and a church that simply is located in the downtown area but pretty much ignores its environment. Likewise we are seeing churches that are not in the central business district carrying out the kind of program we usually associate with a downtown church.

"To be more specific," continued the visiting church planner, "I believe it is helpful if we think in terms of types of 'First Churches' and pay less attention to whether or not the building is located in the central business district, in another part of the city, or in a suburban community. We all recognize that the 'First Church' for a denomination in any community may not actually be named 'First Church.' Likewise we now are beginning to see that the parish that fills the role of 'First Church' not only may not be named First Church; it may not even be located in the central business district."

"I still don't get the relevance of what you're saying to us here at First Church." persisted Mr. Jackson.

"This leads us to two questions," replied their guest. "First, is this really the 'First Church' here, or is another parish filling that role? Perhaps that fifteen hundred-member church over on the east side? Is St. Luke's now really First Church for your denomination? Second, what do you see as your role here in the downtown area?"

"I can answer the first question very easily," spoke up the chairman of the committee. "St. Luke's over on the east side is simply an overgrown neighborhood church. We're still the 'First Church' of our denomination in this town. As far as your second question is concerned, that's why we asked you to meet with us. What is our role? What are our alternatives?"

"You have several alternatives open," was the response. "One alternative is to concentrate on a ministry *to* the people in the central business district. This includes the residents of the area, the persons employed here, and the visitors to the area. This might include a daily noontime worship service, counselling, perhaps specialized programs for specialized groups of people, and possibly courses of instructions for those who need or want them. Here you can exploit your location to maximize the number and variety of your contacts with people."

"Could you give us an example of what you mean?" asked Mr. Wallace.

"Certainly! The First Presbyterian Church of Pittsburgh is

a downtown church of this type. Their Tuesday Noon Club for Businessmen averages eight hundred in attendance for a twenty-five minute noontime program with lunch served both before and afterward. On Thursday noon there is a similar service for businesswomen. On Thursday evening a professional women's group meets at the church. Wednesday is the meeting day for the Mother's Club which studies family life and interpersonal relations from a Christian perspective. There are dozens of groups and classes for every age and interest group covering everything from ceramics to current events, from baby-sitting to book reviews. In a typical week seven thousand persons will enter that downtown church."

"That's quite a contrast with this church," remarked Robert Jackson. "I doubt if a thousand people enter this building each week, and many weeks it probably is fewer than five hundred."

"I am not suggesting that you model yourself after the First Presbyterian Church of Pittsburgh," said their visitor. "I mention this church only as an illustration of one type of downtown church which has done a remarkable job of maximizing the advantages of its location to reach and serve a huge number of people. It has a large membership and many resources; it effectively challenges its members to serve Christ through his church, *and* it provides many unique opportunities for the members to carry out their ministry. The whole venture, I should add, is built on a solid theological foundation, and much of the programming is developed around the small-group principle.

"Another alternative is for a downtown church to look around, see what major needs are left unmet, and then specialize in this one area. In Fort Wayne, for example, the Wayne Street Methodist Church carries on much of the programming normally found in a downtown church of a thousand members. In addition, however, this church has decided to specialize in a ministry to young adults. Fort Wayne has many trade and vocational schools which attract high school graduates from a large area. There are over five thousand of these young adults in the downtown area, and many of them are away from home for the first time in their lives. This church, in cooperation with the denomination and other parishes, has decided to specialize in seeking out and ministering to members of this group of young adults and to help them in their quest for a meaningful, Christian life in the twentieth century."

"How about the great pulpit churches? Is that a separate type?" asked the chairman of the committee.

"There are still a few of these around," replied their visitor, "but the number has declined greatly in the past half-century. Really what you're asking about is a third type of downtown church which seeks to carve out a unique role for itself by excelling in one or two of the traditional program areas. Once we had many great preaching churches, but radio and television have provided deadly competition for the great pulpit figures. Now the pattern is for the 'First Church' in this category to seek to have the highest quality music program in town, or the best Christian education program, or perhaps the best preacher. Others may pick a different area of specialization. One church I know, for example, devotes most of its discretionary resources to sponsoring an outstanding school of religion that runs from September to May. Three or four nights a week and on most Sunday afternoons they have out-standing individuals from all over the world leading classes or giving lectures in their field of competence. These range from theology to missions, from Christian art to leadership training. Their downtown location, their new building, and their large parking lot make this a feasible alternative. Over two thirds of the people who take advantage of their offer-ings are not members of their church.

"Another distinctive type of downtown parish is the church that seeks to play an important role in the community de-cision-making process. Usually it is the pastor and a relatively small group of laymen who are actually involved, but their activity and high visibility tend to give the church a distinc-tive image in the city. This image is reinforced if the church itself displays initiative and leadership. In recent years the number of churches that have attempted to fill this role has increased. Most of them have highly visible programs in social action and provide important community leadership in the peace movement or race relations or antipoverty programs or community organization or urban renewal or housing or political education.

"A fifth type of downtown church is the parish that sees itself as the base for a variety of different operations. One such church is built around a more or less conventional parish ministry with members drawn from all parts of the metro-politan area. In addition to the normal member-oriented program, this church also attempts to encourage a closer relationship between its members and the rest of the church and the world."

"I'm not sure I understand what you mean by this," commented a member of the committee.

"Let me give you three illustrations of what one such First Church does," responded the visiting planner. "They have four full-time professional staff members. One of these is a minister who spends perhaps 10 percent of his time with the congregation. The other 90 percent he spends on the streets and in the bars in one of the roughest parts of town. He is a pastor to the pimps, the prostitutes, the winos, the alcoholics, the homeless, and the hopeless in that part of the city. He not only carries on a significant ministry there; he is a living bridge between that world and the world in which the members of the church reside. This church also is the focal point for most denominational activities in that part of the state. The denominational executive and his assistant have their offices in that church, and a large proportion of the denominational meetings are held there. Thus the church emphasizes its tie with the denomination. In addition to these denominational gatherings, this parish also encourages other groups to use its building. The church houses a day nursery for neighborhood children, provides space for a <u>Planned Parenthood clinic</u>, and provides for scores of meetings. In a typical week such groups as the council of churches, the citizen's housing committee, a civil rights group, and the chamber of commerce might use the church facilities for meetings. Many of the members are deeply involved in the activities of these organizations. This church also has another full-time staff person who spends about half of his time helping the members become involved in a variety of community activities. He knows just about everyone in town and is constantly recruiting people to serve on this committee or to help in that venture. The senior minister calls him a 'broker in civic causes,' since he is always bringing together the people who need volunteers with those who need the opportunity to serve. Last week, for example, he arranged for one of the retired men in the congregation to become the part-time secretary of the Negro Ministerial Alliance.

"Another type of downtown church is the one which concentrates on serving a relatively small geographical parish. In most cities this means serving a very diverse group of people; this can provide an excellent opportunity for the church to fulfill its purpose as a reconciling force. This is one of the least spectacular types of downtown parishes, but often it is one of the most important," concluded the church planner.

"Are you suggesting that we should pattern ourselves after one of these types of downtown churches?" inquired the chairman of the committee.

"Not at all!" responded their visiting consultant. "All I am trying to do is to stimulate your thinking by offering some examples of what other churches are doing in situations somewhat similar to yours. You have to decide for yourselves what your role is in this community."

"Could you help us move toward a decision by boiling all this down to a few simple ground rules for a downtown church?" asked Ed Maloney who had listened in silence up to this point.

"I'm not sure I can do that," replied the church planner, "but I can point out a few things that have impressed me as I have worked with the 'First Church' type of parish.

"First of all, I believe the First Church congregation should listen carefully to discover if there is a special or distinctive role which the Lord is calling it to fill. Usually this distinctive role is not oriented primarily toward the members, but rather toward the community as a whole.

"Closely related to this is the matter of resources. The typical First Church usually has the institutional resources, size, and strength necessary to undertake certain tasks which are outside the realm of possibility for most parishes. Add to these resources some imaginative and creative thinking, and the result is that First Church can become a very exciting place. The problems of such a church are best summarized in the last sentence of Luke 12:48.

"Third," continued their visitor, "we often find that people who join First Church do so for different reasons than those who join the typical parish. For example, one survey of First Churches found that about 15 percent of the people said that the church program was the primary reason for selecting that church. In similar surveys of other churches this figure usually ranged from 4 to 8 percent. The same survey revealed that about 30 percent listed the pastor as the primary reason for joining that church. In the surveys of other parishes this percentage was only half as large."

"You're saying that in a First Church type of parish, pastoral leadership and program are more important in attracting new members than in the typical parish?" asked the chairman.

"Our surveys indicate that this is the case," was the response. "Denominational loyalty seems to be appreciably lower among members of First Churches, and they also tend to transfer from another local church to First Church somewhat more often than the average member transfers his membership locally.

"A fourth point is that the First Churches that have struck me as being especially creative and effective have a certain distinctive flair about them. They tend to be open to innovation, receptive to change, alert to new ideas, and willing to undertake new ministries.

"The last comment I would make in response to your question is that First Churches have to be especially careful to maintain a person-centered attitude. It is very easy for any institution to become object-oriented in its decision-making process and to become more concerned about itself and its property than about the people it is trying to serve. First Churches are especially vulnerable at this point, but they need not yield to this temptation.

"Let me give you a few simple examples of what I mean," he continued. "In one First Church the trustees had always ordered the use of a dirt-colored paint for all the interior painting. They pointed out that the use of this color reduced maintenance costs. They didn't have to wash the walls or repaint as often as they would if they used another color. A few years ago this congregation went through a renewal experience that has changed the whole outlook of the members. One of the minor, but most highly visible, results of this is that the walls are now painted in bright pastel colors. The trustees are now primarily concerned with making this a bright, cheerful, and inviting place for people and are less concerned about maintaining the building at the lowest possible cost.

"In another First Church the program is determined not by the needs of the people, but for the convenience of a few individuals. This is a downtown church with an excellent building at an outstanding location. There are dozens of ways this church could carry on a vital ministry to the people who live, work, and visit in the central business district. What's happened? The church is locked up at five o'clock nearly every afternoon of the week. When I asked why, it turned out that the chief custodian feels he is too old to stay out at night, and he doesn't trust his younger assistant to lock up later. The trustees have gone along with this because they feel that if they let a lot of groups use the building things will get out of hand and their maintenance costs will go up. Outside of a Tuesday noon worship service, the building is used almost entirely for member-oriented activities, and these are confined largely to Sunday morning and Wednesday evening.

"In another large and very famous First Church a self-study committee discovered that 47 percent of the budget was being allocated to maintain the building, and only 21 percent was being spent on program. In this case the congregation became very disturbed and insisted that the program should be given at least as large an allocation of money as the building received. The members concluded that if they were paying that much money simply to operate the building, it would be good stewardship to increase the funds for programming and thus get more use out of the building in ministering to people."

"If I understand you correctly, you're saying that unless we're careful, we will be concentrating our efforts on maintaining the institution rather than on serving people," spoke up Mr. Wallace. "We have the same problem in our department stores. Some of our employees are more interested in maintaining neat-looking display counters than they are in selling the merchandise."

"Every large institution has the same problem," added Mr. Jackson. "I'm on the library board, and some of our staff members spend more time worrying about the appearance of the books and the buildings than they do about increasing circulation. They just can't believe that the library is in business to get the books off the shelves and into people's hands. This is a form of institutional blight, and we have it here at First Church. Many of our members worship this building rather than God, and they're more concerned about maintaining the institution than with serving people."

"Can we overcome this problem that you describe?" asked Ed Maloney. "Or are you suggesting that institutionalism will kill the church?"

"While it is true that what Mr. Jackson described as institutional blight can bankrupt a business or kill a local church, that does not mean institutionalism is bad," replied the council's church planner. "Institutionalism is neither good nor bad in itself. In our complex society we need institutionalized structures, and we need the institutional expression of the church. If the church had not developed some of its highly institutionalized forms and structures, it would be far less effective than it is. As society becomes more complex, the institutions of the church must become more highly developed and more sophisticated. The need is not to prevent the institutionalization of the church; the need is to control it, to view institutionalism as a means and not as an end. We have to stay alert to the dangers of institutional blight, but the way to prevent it is not to destroy the institution."

"How do we prevent institutional blight from ruining our church?" persisted Mr. Maloney.

"The best answer I know," replied the visiting planner, "is to concentrate on a person-centered approach in everything you do. In every decision the goal should be to serve people. Maintaining and improving the institution are only means for achieving that goal. It is not an end in itself.

"The most remarkable example of this I know," he continued, "is in a First Church where the minister has encouraged everyone to develop the attitude that people are really important. When you walk in that church or when you talk with that pastor, you come away feeling that here is a church that truly believes people are important. This is a large congregation with large property holdings, and it is a complex institution, but it is a completely person-centered operation. In that church the blight of institutionalism is not a serious threat."

"This has been helpful," commented the chairman of the committee. "Are there any other challenges or opportunities that you see for a church such as ours?"

"The more I see, the more I am convinced that the greatest challenge to the church in general, but especially to downtown churches, is a ministry to young adults. We know that there is a very sharp decline in participation by young people in the life of the local church when they drop out of or graduate from high school. Most churchmen tend to blame the youngsters for this, and in general the churches write off this group until they grow older, marry, and settle down. Then we welcome them back into the parish church. I believe this is a serious mistake. A more accurate description of what really happens is that we tend to structure our parish programming to serve families, and when young people leave the family nest, we chase them out of the church by ignoring them and their distinctive needs. Very few parishes make a serious and realistic effort to reach this age group. We expect them to participate in our family-oriented programming, and if they don't, we conclude that it is their fault, not ours, that they are dropouts from the church.

"Several churches have been able to reach young adults. They do it by planning their approach specifically to meet the needs of these young people. The downtown church is in an enviable position to do this. Usually it has the location, the resources, the leadership, *and* the opportunities necessary to accomplish this. Often it means a program outside the regular structure, often outside the building, of the downtown church. Young adults are eager to be challenged to carry out the ministry of the church, and therefore many of these efforts have a very heavy service emphasis. Frequently they meet apart from the regular congregation for corporate worship, and usually their study and discussion groups are separate from the traditional church school programming. Incidentally, don't overlook this desire by young people for autonomy and for having their own separate programming.

"Many of the young adults in these ventures do not come from families in that church. Their parents may be members of another parish in a different part of the city or in another part of the country. Most of these young people have left home, symbolically, if not in fact, and they are not attracted by the conventional programming of their home church. While they say they want something 'different,' often in fact they are very conservative. The ministries to this age group that focus on service, study, and worship, *and* that *require* a high degree of participation by these young adults in the planning and execution of all three of these elements of their program are reaching these people. I firmly believe that most downtown churches are in an excellent position to do this and to reach this age group."

"Maybe that is something we should really give serious consideration," commented Mr. Wallace. "There are hundreds of young people fresh out of school coming to this city every year to get a job. A great many live in or near the central business district, and all of them could get to our church very easily, either by car or by bus. There are probably a couple of hundred living within reasonable walking distance. Perhaps we should think in terms of a separate, largely autonomous ministry to this age group."

"We can talk about that later," interrupted Ed Maloney. "I want to hear any other ideas our consultant may have before he has to leave."

"Another opportunity for the downtown church is to make use of the news media, not simply for publicizing its own activities, but on behalf of the entire church," continued the visiting planner. "The high visibility of the downtown church and its central location make its pulpit a potential focal point for the entire community. Combine this potential with the fact that news is comparatively scarce for the Sunday evening television newscasts and for the Monday morning editions of the local newspaper, and this provides a challenging opportunity for the downtown church with a bit of imagination and a sense of mission. Here is a chance for the prophetic word of the church to be heard, not just by those in the building, but by the entire community. A guest preacher on Sunday morning or a special program on Sunday afternoon or evening can present this message to thousands of people. The prophetic word is always news, perhaps never more so than today. Recognition of this fact of timing plus a little careful preparation will enable First Church to make an important witness via the commercial news media.

"In addition to taking advantage of the news vacuum on Sunday evening and Monday morning," continued their guest, "a downtown church has both the opportunity and the need to carry on an effective public relations program to let the entire community know what it is doing and *why*. In a large congregation the task of good internal communication is difficult. As you make a prophetic witness in the larger community and as you tell your story to the whole city, you also are helping your members to see what is happening in their parish. Too often our churches ignore the biblical injunction, and we hide our light under a bushel. All our churches should be less secretive about what they are doing and make greater efforts to let the world see and hear what is happening in the church. The downtown church has some unique advantages in achieving this goal."

"Do you have any advice to offer on staff for a church such as ours?" asked Robert Jackson.

"It is difficult to be specific when I know so little about your situation here," was the reply, "but I can offer four generalizations about staff for First Churches.

"First of all, most large downtown churches have, need, and can afford a multiple staff. Many churchmen, both lay and clergy, oppose this. I don't. One of the strengths of a large downtown church is that it has the money to staff many different ministries.

"Second, I believe in specialization. Rarely would I favor a staff of two or three or four or five ministers each with similar training, interests, and skills. One minister may specialize in community involvement, another in working with young adults, and a third in pastoral calling. One of the most important persons is one we sometimes call an 'enabler.' This is the person who has the skill to help, to assist, to enable laymen to undertake and carry out tasks which frequently are either neglected or left to a paid staff member. In terms of a discipline, such a person's skill is in leadership recruitment and training, but he actually does more than this. He helps each person develop his own potential as a minister of Christ. This enabler not only helps members develop the self-confidence and skills necessary to carry out their responsibilities within the parish; but more important, he helps them perfect their ability to carry on their ministry in the world.

"If one thinks that one of the 'products' of the local church is loving Christians, the enabler is a person who helps to open the doors that enable the members to grow and to realize their God-given potential. While these people are not easy to find, I believe every large church should have a staff member with this skill as an enabler.

"A third generalization, and perhaps the most important, lies in what I said earlier about the vulnerability of a large church to be so concerned with its property that it neglects its program. As a general rule of thumb, I suggest that expenditures for staff and program costs should be at least as large as expenditures for building. Too often we build and maintain buildings and then have very little money left over for staffing a program.

"Finally, I am convinced that in nearly all large parishes everyone, and especially the staff members, needs to know who is the senior minister. In a few situations with the right personnel it is possible to have a team ministry where no one individual is recognized as *the* minister. In the vast majority of parishes, however, I am convinced that the most effective arrangement is to have one man clearly designated as the pastor of the church. I will always remember the remark of a pastor who commented on his experience when he was called to serve as one of the two men in what the church described as a 'dual ministry.' His reaction to this experience was, 'They made a mistake in their spelling. This was really a duel—not a dual—ministry.' "

"All these dreams you have described for us cost money," commented one member of the committee. "How do you suggest a downtown church finance all these activities? Should we try to increase our endowment? This church has about $260,000 in its endowment fund. If we could build this up to a million dollars or so, it would be a big help in financing our work, wouldn't it?"

"This is a much more complicated set of questions than you may realize," was the reply, "First of all you do need adequate financing to carry out your responsibilities. I realize this. In the vast majority of churches this is best done through current receipts from the contributions of the members, not from the earnings of an endowment fund.

"I also realize that a downtown church is an expensive

operation. For example, in the typical urban church it costs about $1 every time someone walks in the door. By this I mean that if you take all the expenditures of the parish except benevolences and divide that figure by the combined total attendance at all activities and services in the church, you will find that it usually averages out to between $.75 and $1.25 every time someone attends any meeting, activity, program, or gathering in the church. By contrast in the typical First Church this averages out to between $1.50 and $2.50 per person. There are obvious limitations to this method of costing out church activities, but this illustrates my point that on a unit cost basis a downtown church is a more expensive operation.

"On the other hand, the giving level in the typical First Church usually is much higher than in other Protestant churches. In the typical urban church, receipts for all purposes including benevolences usually average between $150 and $200 per year times the average attendance at the Sunday morning worship services. In First Church this figure usually averages between $200 and $300, and often is higher than that. In other words, in the typical First Church unit costs are higher, and the giving level is higher. Maybe there is a cause-and-effect relationship here that should be explored, but that is another subject.

"All this leads me to say that I believe in most situations it is possible to finance the operation of the parish from the contributions of the members without depending on the proceeds of an endowment fund. If the income from an endowment fund is used creatively, the fund can be a real asset and enable a congregation to be more effective in fulfilling its basic purpose. In some churches this does happen. The endowment fund finances creative person-centered ministries that would not be possible without this special source of income.

"Far more often, however, the endowment fund becomes a tyrant. Instead of enlarging the list of alternatives open to the congregation and increasing the freedom of the church, it dictates decisions. Instead of supplementing the financial resources of the congregation, the endowment fund stiffles giving. People know the church has this source of income, and they tend to limit their own current giving. Instead of being a creative element in the decision-making process, the endowment fund becomes a blighting influence. Instead of encouraging the church to undertake new person-centered ministries, the endowment fund encourages object-oriented thinking. Gifts to the endowment fund often are designated for care of the building or some similar object-centered use rather than for person-centered ministries. Once an endowment fund has been created, there often develops an unquenchable urge to enlarge it and thus to ensure the security of the church. This desire to buy security for the church is the worst form of institutional blight; it represents the sinfulness of man, the desire for self-sufficiency and alienation from both God and society. This leads to the risk that the congregation will begin to place a higher priority on survival than on service, and on building rather than on program."

"I gather that you would not urge a church to concentrate on building up its endowment fund," remarked Mr. Maloney drily.

"That's the understatement of the day!" was the response.

"Please do not misunderstand me, however. I am not opposed to endowment funds for church-related colleges or hospitals or denominational mission boards. That is another story. I am only opposed to endowment funds in parishes. There, I believe, they may become deadening forces. If I had my way, I would ask every parish to convey its endowment fund to the denominational board of missions or to a hospital or college."

"Frankly, I had hoped you would come in today and lay out a specific course of action for us here at First Church to follow," said the chairman of the committee. "The generalizations you have offered have been interesting, provocative, and helpful, but I am a little disappointed that you weren't more directive. From what you say, I gather you believe it is not possible for you to map out a specific program for us in this church."

"Not only is it not possible, but even if I had that amount of wisdom, it would not be desirable," responded the visiting church planner. "The only good plan for this church's future is the one you develop yourself. All I can do is to offer some advice on specific issues and a few generalizations drawn from experience."

"When this meeting began, we specifically asked what's ahead for *this* church," pointed out Bob Jackson. "I understand your point about the need for us to do our own planning, but what are your reactions to our situation? From your experience and perspective, what do you see here that seems important?"

"I think it is very significant that the congregation has twice rejected proposals to leave the central business district," replied the visitor. "This provides a clear mandate to you to develop plans based on the premise that this will be a downtown church. This means a unique and distinctive role for this church in this city. These two votes could be construed as a mandate to this committee to be innovative and daring in its thinking. To me it is perfectly obvious that this church does not have a long-term future here if it is to be only a convenient and comfortable meeting place for the members. If I were you, I certainly would interpret these two decisions not to move as a mandate to develop some new and exciting proposals for ministry by this church.

"Another important consideration is that your pastor is retiring. This suggests that you should develop a comprehensive statement of purpose and goals before you begin looking for a new minister. In a sense this statement of purpose and goals will form the basis for the job description, not only for your next pastor, but also for other staff members.

"Perhaps you should begin to inquire about the image of this church in the community. How do other people view this church? Does this church have a reputation for being outstanding in any area of ministry? Is that reputation based on current activities, or is it a carry-over from yesterday? What do the pastors in the other First Churches see when they look at this church? How do the members of other parishes in your denomination view this church? What is their image of your church? You might go over the guest register out in the narthex and follow up on the visitors who live in town and never come back. Were some of these visitors newcomers to town who were 'shopping' for a church? Why did they reject this church? Did they join elsewhere?

"If you haven't already done so, you should do a study of your budget, of your evangelistic efforts, and of the capacity of this congregation to assimilate newcomers. In looking over the material you sent me, I asked myself several questions, but I couldn't answer them from the data I had. What percentage of your budget is for the operation and maintenance of the building? How much for mission and witness? How much for benevolence giving? How many new members do you receive on profession of faith each year? What percentage of your members joined during the past three years? What percentage of your leaders joined during the past three years? What are you doing to provide leadership to the general community?

"Finally, I am curious about what you see as the greatest unmet needs in this city. What are these needs? Can this church help meet these needs? What are the resources this parish can muster to meet these needs? What will be the reactions of the members to new and unusual ministries?"

"Just when I thought you had begun to help us answer some of our many questions, you suddenly double the length of our list of unanswered questions," interrupted Mr. Wallace. "But perhaps this is what we need, to first develop a list of the right questions, and then to answer them."

"That's right," agreed their guest. "The questions you ask and the answers you develop to these questions will be far more influential in determining what's ahead for this church than will be the comments of any outsider who is just passing through."

7

What Is Ahead for Yesterday's Congregation?

"What are your goals for the coming year? What is going to be the major thrust of your efforts during the next several months? What do you see as the biggest challenge before you as a church?" These questions were asked by the district superintendent of the quarterly conference of a small Methodist church in western New York state. He was serving his first year on the district and had decided that he would use the subject of goals for the coming year as the major theme for his autumn visits to the churches in his district. He felt that this would help him get acquainted with the congregations and also would stimulate some creative thinking among the leaders of each church.

The church he was visiting on this particular evening was located in the open countryside about six miles from the county seat. The church property consisted of a ninety-year-old white frame one-room structure with a full basement. It was located on a 200-by-200-foot parcel of land lying between the road and a well-filled cemetery. The sanctuary, with pews seating perhaps 150, occupied all the first floor, while the basement was divided into three rooms—kitchen, furnace room, and a large space that served as a fellowship hall, a Sunday school room, and a general meeting place.

The church reported a membership of thirty-three members, an average attendance of twenty-one at worship and eighteen in the Sunday school. During the previous year receipts totalled $1,663 of which $141 was allocated to benevolence giving and $800 (plus $200 for car allowance) was paid the retired minister who supplied the church. During the previous year there had been no baptisms reported and no new members, but three members had been removed by death. Up until two years ago this church had been the "out point" for the 650-member Methodist church located in the nearby county seat town. When it had changed its Sunday morning schedule to include two worship services, the circuit was divided. The county seat church became a full-time appointment, and a newly retired minister who was moving to the county seat agreed to supply the rural church until something else could be worked out. It gave him something to do, and the salary, although modest, was a welcome supplement to his pension and social security checks.

The quarterly conference was being held in the fellowship hall in the basement of the church, and in addition to the pastor and the superintendent nine members of the congregation were present.

There was a long, awkward silence after the superintendent asked about the goals for the coming year. He kept pressing for a response, and finally the lay leader spoke up and said, "I guess our number one goal is to keep the doors open so there can be at least one more quarterly conference held here."

A couple of other members quickly followed up this statement with similar comments. They were concerned primarily with the survival of their church. They knew it was only a matter of time before their present pastor would be unable to continue to supply the pulpit. Where would they be able to find a replacement? The people in the county seat had made it plain that they would talk merger, but they would not consider being part of a circuit once again. What if something happened to the building? What if they had to buy a new furnace? Would the conference come to their assistance? After all, over the years they had given a lot of money to the conference and never received one penny back. In addition, during the past half-century two young men from this church had gone into the ministry. Surely the conference owes this congregation some help, doesn't it?

This story, or one similar to it, can be duplicated hundreds of times in a score of denominations. It can be duplicated many times in New York state and in every state in the nation. It can be duplicated in every large city in America as well as in hundreds of rural counties.

This is the story of yesterday's congregation. This is the story of the church that yesterday met a very important need in its community. This is the story of a rural Lutheran parish in Minnesota, of a Romanian Baptist church in Chicago, of a Hungarian Reformed church in Akron, of a German Evangelical church in Milwaukee, of a declining Church of Christ congregation in an overchurched small town in Texas, of an old, tired Caucasian Presbyterian congregation in Los

Angeles, and of a declining Methodist church in Miami. This is the story of the congregation that yesterday was a vigorous, vital, evangelistic, and active parish, but today appears to have no future. This is the story of the parish that reached its peak in terms of membership and institutional strength in the 1920's—or perhaps in the 1950's or 1960's—and has been declining ever since that date. This is the story of thousands of congregations which today are functionally obsolete.

What happened? Why are over fifty of these congregations disappearing from the· scene every week? Why are there so many of these parishes that are oriented toward yesterday rather than tomorrow? Why are there so many congregations that are so wrapped up in the struggle to survive that they have no resources left for service?

While the reasons are many and do vary from one situation to another, most of these churches fall into one of three general categories.

Who Are Yesterday's Congregations?

The first group is composed of those parishes that were organized to fill a special need, and then the passage of time eliminated that need.

This group includes the thousands of rural churches that were organized decades ago when this was primarily an agricultural nation, when the means of transportation were limited, and when the residents of a rural community supplied many of their own needs. The organizational counterpart to the rural church was the one-room country school.

The decline of the farm population—it dropped from 32,-000,000 persons in 1935 to 12,000,000 in 1965—the tremendous improvement in the means of transportation and the revolution of rising expectations spelled the end of the one-room country school. Between 1942 and 1962 the number of school districts in the nation dropped from 108,579 to 34,678. This was a result of consolidations—the same school consolidations that almost completely eliminated the one-room country school.

As these changes came at an ever faster pace, many people felt their church to be the only place that represented a refuge from change, a haven of security, an unbreakable tie with "the good old days," and a place of institutional stability. They clung to their church; they struggled to maintain it and keep it open, but the calendar and economic forces were relentless opponents. Each year members died or moved away, and replacements were few and far between. The result has been that an estimated 2,000 to 3,000 rural churches close each year; but for each one that closes, there are ten fighting valiantly against overwhelming odds to stay alive.

In this same category with the open-country rural churches are the parishes in the tiny crossroad villages that once were the trading centers for mining and farming communities. Such a village may once have included a couple of hundred residents, three or four churches, a high school, two or three grocery stores, a garage, a hardware store, a couple of taverns, and a blacksmith shop. The tractor eliminated the blacksmith. The hard-paved roads and the automobile enabled the competition from the city a dozen miles away to wipe out most of the merchants, and consolidation closed the high school. Only the churches held out against change.

The second group of churches is largely, but not entirely, urban. These parishes were established to minister to a special ethnic or cultural group. The most highly visible were those that ministered to a special group of immigrants and conducted the worship services in German, Finnish, Italian, Spanish, or some other foreign language. Less visible, but very numerous, were those parishes that relied on English as the language and were made up of families in which the adults came from another part of the world—perhaps from the British Isles or from some part of rural America where the religious subculture was different from that encountered in the big city. The passage of time, the immigration legislation of the 1920's, the depression of the 1930's, the Americanization of the children, and the decentralization of the urban population gradually have added up to the demise of many of these congregations that were established before 1941.

(The renewed immigration from rural America during and following World War II and the new wave of immigration from abroad during the late 1950's and the 1960's have resulted in the establishment of thousands of similar new congregations in the large cities of America. In another generation many of these new congregations, which today have a high degree of relevance, will join the ranks of yesterday's congregations.)

The third category of yesterday's congregations is composed of those parishes that have simply become irrelevant to the contemporary world—not because of the changes that occurred in the world outside the church doors as happened

to so many rural congregations, nor because of the accultura-
tion of their clientele as happened in the thousands of ethnic
parishes, but because of the changes that occurred within the
congregation itself.

These are the congregations that have changed, usually
very gradually, from an open, evangelical, Christian fellowship into a closed, self-centered, backward-looking group
primarily concerned with preservation of the institution.

Frequently these congregations lost their sense of evangelism
when they decided that the newcomers to the neighborhood
were "different" and were not acceptable as members. These
"differences" usually were based on variations in ethnic background, race, color, education, income, occupation, language,
and similar irrelevant distinctions.

An examination of the life cycles of churches in these
three categories and a comparison with the many parishes
that are vital, evangelical, open, forward looking, neighbor-
centered congregations lead to the development of several
generalizations.

Most obvious of all is a lesson taught by Jesus. "For who-
ever would save his life will lose it" (Matt. 16:25). This is
true not only for men, but also for institutions and especially
for churches. Self-centeredness is the way of destruction for
every person and every institution.

Closely related to this is the realization that the seed of
death is in every institution and in every church, just as every
person knows that someday he is going to die. For the parish
church the inevitability of death often is ignored until it is too
late. How soon death comes is determined by the members of
the parish. Many parishes die after a generation or two;

others live for centuries. The seed of death is in every parish, however, and it is only a question of time before that local church passes from the scene.

There are some churchmen who cannot see this. They know the promise that the reign, the mercy, and the righteousness of the Lord is forever and ever. From this they presume that their local church has been promised life everlasting.

This myth of the indestructibility of the institutional expression of the church lives on despite a mounting pile of evidence to the contrary. For examples of the vulnerability of the institutional expression of the church, one can look to the shores of North Africa where Christianity once flourished and see that today this is now a stronghold of Islam. Or one can turn to Geauga County in northeastern Ohio where an enterprising local historian found that three fourths of the religious congregations that had been organized in that county had disappeared over the space of 130 years.

Thus the question is not *if* a local church is going to pass from the scene, but rather *when, why,* and *how.* Over a generation ago H. Paul Douglass, Ross Sanderson, and other students of the parish church pointed out that adaptability to change was the most important factor in the survival of the church as a servant congregation or even for survival as an institution.

As an illustration of this truth an untold number of ethnic and language congregations have changed and adapted to changing conditions, and today are effective and relevant parishes. Instead of being described as yesterday's congregations, they are a significant element in the contemporary religious scene in their communities. Likewise many rural and small-town congregations have adapted to change and also continue as strong, vital, neighbor-centered parishes. A great many other churches, instead of drifting into the third category of yesterday's congregations described earlier, also have adapted to change and continue as relevant and important religious forces.

When the question of *why* some parishes have failed to adapt to changing conditions is asked, there appears to be no single answer. In some cases the primary responsibility can be assigned to pastoral leadership, in others to lay leadership. In some parishes where adaptation to change did occur, one of the causes was the availability and exploitation of denominational resources, especially the advice, expertise, and guidance in planning, decision making, and implementation of decisions. Therefore it is only fair to assume that in some of what have become yesterday's congregations, it was the absence or the unavailability of this denominational assistance that made the difference.

Signs of Death

Another way of answering the *why* question is to examine some of the characteristics of congregations that appear to be dying. These are not only the common characteristics of yesterday's congregation; they also help explain *why* a parish may be in the last stage of its life cycle.

The most highly visible of these characteristics is the lack of outreach and an almost total concentration of resources on member-oriented activities. This lack of balance in the concept of purpose, described more fully in chapter 1, is an overemphasis on the care of the congregation. Evangelism and outreach, mission and witness in the world are almost completely ignored, especially when measured in terms of the allocation of lay leadership.

A second characteristic is an excessive emphasis on the past. Frequently this is expressed by the celebration of a large number of anniversaries, homecomings, and other events which glorify the past. When the effort that goes into preparing for these exceeds the effort that goes into evangelism and mission, it often is a sign that this has become one of yesterday's congregations. When the largest attendance is registered at one of these events, rather than on Easter Sunday or some other important date on the Christian calendar, it may be a sign that the end probably is not far away for that parish. Sometimes this nostalgic longing for the past is expressed as worship of the building. The care and maintenance of the building, rather than the effective use of the building as a tool for mission, become the governing concern of the trustees. This, too, is a mark of yesterday's congregation.

A third sign of a parish in the last stages of its life cycle is the neighborhood church without a neighborhood constituency. Some parishes are not neighborhood churches. The typical First Church and most downtown churches do not function as neighborhood churches and should not be evaluated in terms of a neighborhood constituency. The vast majority of local churches, however, should have a strong neighborhood orientation. The lack of a meaningful relationship to neighboring residents frequently is a characteristic of yesterday's congregation.

A fourth and often regarded as the least important of

these signs is the attitude of the congregation toward the denomination, denominational officials, and denominational resources. Many of what have become yesterday's congregations view the denomination as an enemy rather than as a potential ally. They do not comprehend the nonfinancial assistance that the denomination can provide the local church. The parish that is nearing the end of its era often feels lonely, neglected, and far removed from the denominational family. Instead of viewing the denomination as a source of aid, advice, and help, the denomination is seen as an outside force extracting money from the local church and attempting to dictate policy, program, and goals.

This sense of alienation makes it very difficult for the denomination to render assistance and to help the parish adapt to change. After many bitter experiences, a number of denominational executives have reached the conclusion that the only parishes that should receive assistance are those which seek it and which also present a carefully thought-out brief explaining their purpose, their goals, the type of assistance sought, and how this assistance will help the parish fulfill its purpose. This means that only those parishes which possess the initiative, imagination, and skill to ask for assistance receive it. This is less than a satisfactory result since many of the local churches that need help the most are those which lack the initiative, the imagination, and the skill to seek outside help.

On the other hand, experience strongly suggests that unsolicited help seldom is used effectively. When a denomination offers to pay the cost of an extra staff member to be a neighborhood evangelist, it seldom does much good unless the congregation wants to serve the neighborhood. When a denomination offers to help pay the operating costs of a local church, it seldom does much good unless that parish has first carefully analyzed its resources, its sense of stewardship, its purposes, its program, and its goals. When a denominational staff person comes to meet with a parish committee to discuss problems, plans, needs, and the future, it seldom does much good unless the leaders have first seen the need for this consultation and have asked him to meet with them.

An unknown, but significant, number of parishes that were having difficulty adapting to change have been helped along the road to renewal and relevance through effective use of denominational resources. Many of what now can best be described as yesterday's congregations have ignored this potential source of help.

A congregation displaying only one or two of these four characteristics may or may not belong in the category of yesterday's congregations. A parish displaying all four of these characteristics, however, probably has a short life expectancy as a church. It may continue to exist for years or even decades as an institution, but its future as a *religious* institution is limited.

When Does Death Come?

How long after these signs of death begin to appear does the parish fade from the scene? Are there any statistical measurements that can be used to predict the imminence of death? Are there any distinctive conditions that tend to be present at the time of death? While it is impossible to give precise answers to these questions, three sets of generalizations may provide some helpful insights.

First, once a congregation moves into this final stage of its life cycle, death in the form of dissolution, merger, or relocation often comes with surprising swiftness. Frequently it comes when it appears that the parish still has a large reserve of strength and resources. For example, one congregation began a serious study of its long-term involvement in the life of the community in October. The following March it dissolved. Another, after careful study, concluded that it should begin a ten-year program of outreach in the community. Two years later it decided to relocate. In a third, the leaders met at eight o'clock one evening to begin discussions of a $350,000 building program. Two hours later they decided they had only two alternatives—dissolution or merger.

On the other hand, it should be noted that in many small, weak, struggling congregations the lay leadership appears to be intuitively aware of the fact that once the institution moves into this last stage of the life cycle, death may come very suddenly. Therefore every care is exercised to avoid the challenge or the unusual expenditure of effort that might jeopardize the future of the institution. This can be seen most commonly in rural areas. In observing the functioning of these congregations one is reminded of the frail, eighty-nine-year-old widow who moves with the greatest caution, knowing that a fall may put her into the hospital—and also knowing that the hospital bed will be her death bed.

Second, while they must be used with discretion, it is possible to develop a set of statistical yardsticks that may be helpful in forecasting the imminence of death. When the average attendance at worship is less than 40 percent of the total confirmed membership, when the rate of baptisms each year is less than two per one hundred members, when the number of persons received on profession of faith annually is less than two per one hundred members, when the median age of the membership is twenty years above the median age of the residents of the community, when the level of giving drops to the bottom 10 percent for churches in the denomination in that region, when over 85 percent of the budget is allocated to congregational care, and when over one half of the expenditures are for the care and maintenance of the property, death probably is near.

The third generalization is that in many of the larger parishes (one hundred to five hundred members) which suddenly disappeared from the scene, one or more of these conditions usually prevailed: (1) the death of the parish came *either* soon after the resignation, retirement, or death of a pastor who had served the parish for twenty to fifty years *or* within two years after his successor arrived; (2) the definition of purpose that controlled the decision-making process had shifted from a theological to an institutional base; (3) Negroes or low-income whites or persons from a different subculture had begun to move into the neighborhood around the church; (4) a high degree of pessimism dominated the thinking of the leaders; (5) a noncommittal pulpit had led to a lack of commitment among the members; (6) the dominant concern of the leadership was to secure more members to serve the institution; and (7) unit costs as measured by participation or individuals in the church's program had risen to double or triple the average for parishes in that community.

What Are the Alternatives?

What lies ahead for those congregations that cannot or will not adapt to changing conditions? What is in the future for the parishes that show the symptoms of impending death? What is the future of the thousands of rural churches located in areas of rapidly declining population? What is ahead for the tightly knit German-background urban congregation that looks out one day to discover that nearly all of the younger members of the parish have moved to suburbia and that all of the newcomers to the neighborhood are Negroes? What is going to happen to the small Hungarian congregation that learns that its property is to be purchased by the city as part of an urban renewal project or for construction of a new expressway?

There are four answers that may be given.

The most common, and the least rational, is to hang on as long as possible until the pressures of time and change force the parish to dissolve, merge, or relocate. Eventually the name of this congregation is added to the lengthening list of parishes that have faded from the scene in that neighborhood.

The most creative and most widely discussed answer today is renewal. This is the process of the rediscovery of purpose, the reawakening of a sense of mission, the redefinition of goals, and the renewing of the spirit of the members. This is the process of moving from a survival structure to a missionary structure. This happens. It happens far more often than most critics of the parish realize. It happens in many situations in which denominational executives, church planners, and consultants have completely written off a parish as doomed to extinction. It happens often enough to demonstrate the power of the Holy Spirit. It happens as the result of an infusion of new resources by the denomination, and sometimes it happens without outside assistance.

While this is the most desirable answer to the question in most parishes, this is not always the answer to be sought. In many rural areas and in hundreds of small towns where there has been a 30 or 50 or 70 percent decrease in the population, unilateral efforts at renewal are not the logical goal. Too many of these communities are now so badly overchurched that it would be poor stewardship to try to perpetuate every parish. Likewise many urban parishes cannot be renewed without pouring in an excessive quantity of denominational resources. Frequently it is better, and often far more economical, to organize a new parish to minister to the newcomers than it is to try to encourage and enable some of yesterday's congregations to be renewed.

This leads to a third alternative—death and resurrection. The most common illustration of this process occurs when an urban, or sometimes a suburban, congregation dissolves and turns its property and other assets over to the denomination to be used in the establishment of a new parish. A typical example of this is the fifty- or hundred-year-old dwindling congregation that loses its sense of outreach and mission and concentrates all its resources on congregational care. It is unable to welcome the newcomers to the neighborhood into the fellowship of the parish. As the members die or move away, the strength of the parish diminishes. First comes a request to the denomination for financial assistance in paying the bills. Next comes the realization that what was hoped to be only a temporary disability is actually a fatal illness. Instead of fighting to stay alive until the last nickel of the assets has been spent, the members begin to realize that while a struggling church is an appropriate symbol of Christianity, a dying church is a most inappropriate symbol. They see that they are no longer a struggling parish; they are now a dying church. Instead of waiting for the inevitable, the members vote to terminate their existence as a parish, dissolve, and assign the assets to the denomination to be used for a new ministry in that neighborhood. A new parish arises out of the old.

A somewhat similar pattern can be observed in many rural communities which are seriously overchurched. Two or three or four tiny, struggling congregations may decide to abandon their old institutional forms and come together to form one new parish which is large enough to provide an adequate ministry in that community. Instead of continuing as separate parishes, each devoting most of its resources to the battle for survival, the new parish is large enough to provide an effective ministry to both the members and the larger community. This new parish may be one congregation formed as the result of a merger, or it may be composed of several congregations united in one larger parish. In one sense this may be described as death and resurrection.

The fourth answer is simply death. This is the most difficult of all answers for church members to accept. This is somewhat strange and suggests that a doctrine of death for institutions is needed. Christians have a doctrine of death that helps them understand and accept the death of a loved one, but the church has yet to develop a doctrine of death for institutions.

Any suggestion to close a Protestant church usually is greeted by such a quantity and variety of objections that the proposal seldom is given a fair hearing. This is most unfortunate, especially in view of the fact that 3,000 to 4,000 churches dissolve or merge every year.

In discussing the future of these parishes where dissolution, merger, or relocation clearly is the appropriate course of action, experience suggests five items that should be on the agenda for the congregational meeting when the members decide to take a realistic look at the future.

First of all, it should be emphasized that this not only is not a dishonorable move, but it may be the most honorable action. Some church members have such strong sentimental ties to the building, the traditions of that parish, or to their parents or grandparents who were leaders in the congregation that they are overcome with guilt feelings when someone suggests closing the church. They need help in seeing that while this church once may have had a necessary and vital place in the community, that need is no longer present. They need help in seeing that some other alternative may provide a more effective and meaningful ministry to the people in that neighborhood. They need help in seeing that it would be poor stewardship to keep the church open. They may need help in seeing that this action is really a step forward, not backward, in building the Kingdom. Dissolving the congregation or merging it with another parish and closing the church may be the most responsible, and therefore the most honorable, course of action.

The second item is closely related to the first—the importance of discussing the purpose, not just for this one particular parish, but of the larger church. How *did* this parish fit into that pattern of purpose? How does it fit *now*? What are the needs *now*? If this church were not here, would it be wise to start it in terms of fulfilling these purposes? What is the balance between the input of resources and the output of ministry?

There also should be plenty of time on the agenda to allow the members to express their emotional reactions to change and the implications of change for the church. This may even require an extra meeting or two, but it can be very helpful for people to unburden themselves. As they articulate their reactions, it helps them understand both *what* is happening and *why* it is happening.

A fourth item is the establishment of a deadline. Instead of letting the closing of the church be an act of resignation, it is far better if it can be scheduled in the form of an act of obedience and submission to the will of God. If the actual closing can be scheduled sometime in advance, this event can be a meaningful religious service. It can recognize the years of faithful service of the parish and also be an act of worship in which faithfulness, obedience, and the continuity of the universal church are emphasized.

Finally, a very important item on the agenda is the need to help the members find a new church home. Too often this is neglected. No one feels it is his responsibility. In most cases this is a denominational responsibility, and the denominational staff should make sure that this matter is considered well in advance of the actual closing. It is very helpful if each member can be offered two or three alternatives.

In discussing what lies ahead for yesterday's congregation, we see that there are no easy answers. Renewal is the most rewarding and certainly the most gratifying, but it is not always the appropriate answer. In many cases it is necessary to recognize realistically that just as changing conditions require the establishment of new parishes in some communities, in other communities these same forces of change spell the end for what yesterday were some of the most vital and significant churches in the nation.

8

What Is Our Strategy?

"George, you know it's about time somebody did something about the housing over on the west end of town," remarked Ed Brown to his friend George Moore as they waited for the waitress to bring their luncheon orders. "I was talking to the fire chief this morning, and he told me there have been four serious fires over there already this winter. You remember the one where the boy and his grandmother were both killed. Well, the chief tells me there were three fires just as bad except no one was injured. In each case someone lost his home and most of his possessions. The people in this town ought to do something."

"You're about the fourth person to mention this subject to me in the last month," responded George Moore, "but let's face the facts. First, there are really just a bunch of shacks over there. When one burns down, it is not much of a loss, so no one is going to get excited. Second, I suspect that about three fourths of them are rented, and the owners aren't going to put any money into that neighborhood—if they have good sense, they won't. Third, even though this is the largest city in the county, we have a population of only about 20,000. My guess is there are about 150 homes over there that should be condemned and razed. If you were to do that and replace each one with a new $12,000 cement-block house, and that is the rock-bottom minimum it would cost, you're talking about an expenditure of $2,000,000. That's an average of $100 for every man, woman, and child in town. This community is not going to put up that kind of money simply to get rid of one nuisance! I'm not very happy about the situation either, Ed, but if you're going to start a crusade, you better pick a less expensive one."

Ed Brown did not forget about it. He talked to a number of other community leaders, but while nearly everyone agreed that conditions were deplorable, no one seemed interested in doing anything about it.

Later that same month Ed was attending a meeting of the Social Action Committee of his church. A few months earlier a new pastor had come to Westminster Church. He had reactivated the group, and they were casting about for something to do. Ed Brown felt this might be the time and place to air his pet peeve. He quickly found that everyone, including the new pastor, knew about the "West End Allotment" as it was called, and everyone agreed that it was a deplorable situation.

One member pointed out that the health and life of the residents were endangered by the housing. Another commented that it was a terrible place to raise children, while a third emphasized that the very existence of such a slum was not only a blight on the whole community, but also a black mark on all the churches of the city that they had tolerated such conditions for so long. How could they preach a Christian doctrine of man and close their eyes to these conditions?

It soon became evident that the members of the committee, with perhaps two exceptions, were ready to join Ed Brown in a crusade that very evening, but what could they do?

After another half hour of expressing their frustrations over their lack of power and their extremely limited resources, one member suggested a course of action.

"When Ed brought up this subject, we all knew what he was talking about," began Mrs. Russell, a dynamic and attractive young housewife, "but none of us had ever thought about it to the point that we became disturbed. As we talked, we all became concerned, or maybe I should say our consciences began hurting. What we need to do is to make this problem the topic of discussion for a lot more people. If a lot more consciences are troubled, maybe something will happen.

"Perhaps what we could do," she continued, "is to survey the area. Let's find out just how many shacks there are in that allotment, how many people do live there, and what the real conditions are."

That very evening five members of the committee volunteered to undertake the responsibility for the survey. They went out and counted the houses in the allotment. At the courthouse they compiled a list of the owners and the assessed valuation of the individual parcels of property. They visited the fire and police departments and the welfare office and secured statistical data on some of the social problems of the area. They talked to the principal of the nearby elementary school and the guidance counselor at the high school.

Two months later they made their report to the Social Action Committee of Westminster Church. The survey committee described what they had found and emphasized that they had the material for a series of stories in the local newspapers that would really rock the town.

"Now just a minute," spoke up Jim O'Brien who had not been a member of the volunteer survey team; "before we go off half-cocked, I would like to ask two questions. First, did you talk to any residents of the allotment? Second, do we have a plan of action? Let's not start something that may produce a lot of talk, but no action."

"We didn't make any special effort to interview the residents of the allotment," replied Ed Brown, "and I am not sure what you are suggesting by your question; but you have an excellent point. We must go out and talk with more of the residents. Some of our committee happened to chat with a few people there, but we did not make any systematic effort along these lines. It would be a mistake for us to try to stir up anything until after we had talked to the people involved. That's a very good suggestion!"

"Now how about a plan of action?" prodded Mr. O'Brien. "Do we have anything to talk about in terms of a constructive program?"

"I think Jim has raised an important question," interrupted the pastor. "What he is asking is: Do we have a strategy for changing the situation? Do we? He's absolutely right. Unless we begin now to develop a strategy, we are liable to spark a lot of talk but no action."

During the next hour the air was filled with action proposals. One person suggested petitioning the city to undertake an urban renewal project for the West End Allotment. Another suggested that the church should build new housing to accommodate the residents of the area, while a third argued for a self-help "fix-up and paint-up" program with a minimum of outside assistance. The meeting adjourned with no decision on either a plan of action or a strategy, but with a clear recognition of the need for more study.

After several more meetings and hours of discussion the Social Action Committee of Westminster Church concluded that they had undertaken a four-point program when they decided "to do something" about housing conditions in the West End Allotment.

First, they had agreed on the need to stir up discussion and concern in the entire community about the problem. The survey was a part of that effort. They needed documented facts if they were going to arouse the people from their lethargy and prod the community into action.

Second, they quickly saw the need to talk with the residents of the allotment and find out how they viewed the situation. Talk about "maximum feasible participation of the poor" during the various church programs on poverty and affluence, the growing recognition of the need for indigenous leadership, and a growing understanding of the implications of the Christian doctrine of man—all had a cumulative effect on the members at Westminster. The members of the Social Action Committee recognized the absolute necessity of developing a program *with*, rather than *for*, the residents of the allotment.

Third, with the leadership of Jim O'Brien, the committee members saw the need to do more than simply arouse the community conscience and hope something would happen. Each member of the committee could recall various good ideas that had been advanced and had aroused widespread interest, but most of them had died because of the lack of a specific plan of action for implementation.

Fourth, the committee realistically recognized that regardless of its merit, any plan devised by the Social Action Committee of Westminster Church probably would never be implemented unless it had widespread support.

As they discussed this, the first response was to develop such a good program that it automatically would win the enthusiastic backing of many groups and individuals. This idealistic goal was soon dismissed, however, as the committee members recognized the need for allies. Jim O'Brien made the point clearly when he said, "You know what's a good plan of action? It's a plan that *I* have had a part in developing. In *my* eyes, any plan that *I* have prepared or helped to prepare is better than any plan developed without me."

The pastor endorsed the comment of Mr. O'Brien and added, "There is another side to this, too. While I have great respect for the members of this committee and for their dedication, I don't believe we have a corner on all the wisdom on this subject. By involving other people, we not only are more likely to get their support, but I suspect we just may end up with a better quality plan of action."

The committee concluded that they needed to interest other groups in the community in the problems of the West End Allotment, help them see the urgency of the situation, and then have a broad-based community group develop a plan of action. It also was decided not to go to the newspaper with the results of their survey until after this more inclusive community organization could be formed and had had the opportunity to prepare a program that would improve the housing in the allotment. The information they had gathered would be useful in arousing interest and in securing allies, but they decided they should wait until they developed a coalition and had a constructive program before they went out after headlines. They did not want the effort to die because of a lack of effective follow-through.

At this point the committee began to make a list of groups, organizations, and individuals who should be contacted with the goal of arousing their interest and enlisting their support in developing an action program. The list included the other churches in town, the residents of the allotment, the mayor, the alderman from the west side, representatives from the local service clubs, and the chairman of the city planning commission.

The experience of the Social Action Committee at Westminster Church offers a relevant case study in responding to the question: How do you go about translating ideas into action?

In every church some people develop proposals for improving the current situation. Some are abandoned because of lack of interest. Many fail on their own merits. Others appear to have merit but never move beyond the discussion stage. How can ideas be translated into action? How can change be effected? Is there a systematic method of achieving change? Questions such as these plague many churchmen. The imperative of the Christian gospel compels them to action, but how does one go about getting results, either in the church or in the community?

Persons concerned with the process of social change have studied this subject and have developed answers to these questions. There is a strategy for change; there is a method for turning talk into constructive action; there is a systematic method of mobilizing for action. The basic outline of this strategy is illustrated by the activities of the Social Action Commission at Westminster and by countless other efforts to effect change.[1]

The Place of Discontent

The strategy begins with discontent. If everyone is completely satisfied with current conditions, it will be impossible to achieve planned change. Ed Brown was discontented with the housing condition in the West End Allotment, and this discontent led him to try to do something about it. He made progress only after he found a group of people who shared his discontent. The Social Action Committee recognized that more people would have to become disturbed over this housing problem before anything constructive could be accomplished.

Discontent, however, is not an automatic result of undesirable conditions. Frequently the fires of discontent have to be fanned. People often have to have their attention called to the situation that needs changing before they become aroused to the point of supporting change. Most of the

[1] I am greatly indebted to Christopher Sower, *Community Involvement* (Glencoe: Free Press, 1958) and Professor Karl Hertz of the Hamma School of Theology for the basic outline of the steps in the process of effecting social change. This outline served as a model in developing the analysis presented here.

time most of the people are satisfied, or at least tolerant of the conditions around them.

Frequently a dramatic event is needed to arouse the concern of people to the point that they become discontented and willing to support, or at least accept, changes. The civil rights movement of the early and mid-1960's was sparked by a series of dramatic events which changed the mood of a nation and enabled many overdue changes to take place.

The same point is illustrated by what happened in a small Wisconsin parish a few years ago. For over a generation the Sunday school, with about the same number of persons in attendance, had been meeting in inadequate quarters in the small white-frame church. Three classes met in the basement, two in the sanctuary, one in the Sunday school room on the first floor, and three more in tiny rooms on the floor above the Sunday school room. While no one boasted about the facilities, most of the members of the church were satisfied with the arrangement, and the remaining few apparently were willing to tolerate it because there appeared to be no alternative.

As the years went by, the personnel changed, and eventually eight of the classes were taught by young men and women in their twenties and early thirties. One evening the teachers of these eight classes met, and the next day one of the teachers stopped by to see the pastor and said, "We had a Sunday school teachers' meeting last night, and we decided we wouldn't teach anymore unless we have better physical facilities for carrying on our program of Christian education. I called the church school superintendent this morning to tell him of our decision, and he suggested that I talk to you right away since the official board is scheduled to meet this evening. We really mean it," she added politely in a gentle voice. "Unless something is done, next Sunday is our last Sunday."

Needless to say, the discontent of the Sunday school teachers precipitated a crisis. Many members of the official board who had either attended classes or taught in the Sunday school thought the teachers were being unreasonable, but it seemed even more unreasonable to try to find a dozen new teachers in four days. The reactions of some of the other members were expressed by one person who conceded, "Well, I had never given the matter much thought before, but when you compare our Sunday school facilities with the classrooms in the new consolidated school or with what the Presbyterians and the Lutherans have built recently, I guess maybe we ought to do something." Before adjourning that night the official board had designated a building committee and instructed it to bring in alternative proposals for additional church school facilities. It was hoped that this would mollify the teachers and that they would not carry out their threat to resign.

The discontent of the small group of teachers, dramatically expressed, had been communicated to the official board, and two years later a new combination church school-fellowship hall building was consecrated.

The Role of the Initiators

Discontent is only the prelude to action. Discontent alone does not lead to change; it only sets the stage for those who are the actors in the second step of the process.

Discontent normally leads to discussion of the ways and means to do something about the cause of the discontent. How can we solve this problem? Frequently these discussions constitute both the beginning and the end of this step. In that case the second step becomes the final step, and nothing happens. In other situations, however, the discussants include people who are able and willing to become *initiators*. They are the persons who not only are willing to talk, but who also have enthusiasm and energy. These individuals are willing to take the initiative in developing a plan to solve the problem.

Sometimes these initiators are self-appointed. Ed Brown was a self-appointed initiator (some called him a crusader) in his community. In terms of what eventually happened, the Social Action Committee at Westminster Church was a group of self-appointed initiators. They went far beyond what anyone expected of them when they were elected to serve on that committee.

Sometimes the initiators are officially designated. In the case of the rural church in Wisconsin the Sunday school teachers expressed their discontent and dramatically focused attention on the problem. They did not even suggest a solution. In that situation the initiators, the ones who eventually proposed an acceptable solution, turned out to be the members of the building committee, an officially designated group in the church.

The distinctive characteristic of the initiator is a dedication to the issue in question. This dedication means he will devote the time and energy required to prepare a plan of action. The *effective* initiator also will have the perseverance, the tenacity, the openness, and the receptivity to the suggestions of others that will enable him to see a program through to its implementation.

The Social Action Committee at Westminster revealed an unusual degree of sophistication at this point. They were not only open to the ideas of others; they also decided not to give primary attention to developing a specific solution, but rather to recruit other initiators who could bring both wisdom and support to the issue. They recognized the value of enlarging their group and of maximizing the extent of community participation as early in the process as possible.

Building a Coalition

The people at Westminster were ready and willing to move into the third stage of the change process—building a coalition—before getting bogged down in developing a specific program. In effect, they sought to carry out the second and third steps—initiating a program to solve the problem and developing a network of support—at the same time.

This third step in the process of effecting change is the crucial one. It is one that many groups never take and as a result are frustrated in achieving their goal. Sometimes a group attempts to move directly from the second to the fourth step in this process. This not only illustrates their unawareness of the dynamics of the change process, but it also greatly reduces their chances of guiding the course of change.

Frequently a group is never able to take this third step in the process because of handicaps incurred in the first two steps. They may have placed so much emphasis on the first step, stirring up discontent, that the community is fragmented and polarized to the extent that it is impossible to build a coalition sufficiently broad and powerful to secure the implementation of any positive proposal. It often is relatively easy for any one of the fragments of the divided community to gain sufficient power to veto the program proposed by other segments, and the divisions can be so sharp that there can be no agreement on any one constructive course of action. Or it may be that in the second step the initiators, the persons who accepted the responsibility for developing a solution to the problem, prepared a proposal which cannot win broad support. Sometimes the obstacle is the program; sometimes it is the dogmatic and uncompromising attitude of those who prepared the program.

Attempts to achieve change in the local church are especially vulnerable at this third step of the process. The major reason for this vulnerability is that the local church finds it difficult to act without a consensus. A simple majority usually is insufficient. Therefore any plan for change in a local church in American Protestantism seldom can be implemented unless it has unanimous or near unanimous support. More significant, it almost always can be vetoed by a minority group. Another reason for emphasizing the importance of broad-based support for any proposal for change in a Protestant congregation is the dearly held "right" of withdrawal. The lack of effective church discipline means that any opponent of a proposal may transfer his membership, cut off his financial support, or impose some other form of sanction. In most congregations if more than a couple of active leaders threaten this action, it will block the proposed changes.

Frequently a coalition in support of change cannot be formed in a local church because of what happened in the two previous steps in the process. If the effort to dramatize discontent was overdone, it may have alienated enough members that they constitute a formidable veto bloc. Likewise the efforts of the initiators in the second step may halt the entire change process. Frequently the initiators develop a plan of action which is completely unacceptable to several leaders, and they form a veto bloc. Sometimes the initiators are so sure that they have developed the only practical plan that they refuse to listen to suggestions and thus create a veto group. Occasionally there are too many groups of initiators, and each has developed its own proposal. None will yield, and therefore no single plan is able to secure consensus support.

The members of the Social Action Committee at Westminster Church displayed a commendable awareness of these pitfalls. They were careful not to rush out in search of a few headlines in the newspaper at the risk of alienating potential supporters. Likewise they recognized that they could gain more supporters for action if they left the door wide open for these recruits to share in the preparation of a plan of action. Their subsequent success demonstrated the wisdom of their decisions. On the other hand, it should be noted that there are occasions when this might not be the best strategy. Occasionally it is necessary to place greater emphasis on enlarging the core of people who are discontented with current conditions, even at the risk of alienating some who might otherwise be helpful allies. Frequently it is necessary to prepare at least a specific, although tentative, proposal for change before it is possible to enlist adequate support.

This critical third step of coalition building calls for the inclusion of two kinds of support. It also requires recognition of potential opposition to the proposed program of change.

The two types of support required are legitimation and power. Rarely can any program of change succeed unless it is generally recognized as "the thing to do." This stamp of approval is referred to as *legitimation*. It may be as simple as getting public support of one or two prestigious individuals. It often requires the more time-consuming effort of helping a great many people see that this is the right thing to do at this time. It often is dependent on a national climate of opinion. Ed Brown had long been concerned about the conditions in the West End Allotment, but he did not gain support for his concern until the American conscience had been pricked by the national attack on poverty in the mid-1960's. What had once been a crusade became the proper thing to do.

The second type of support required may be described by the general word "resources" or more simply as *power*. Power comes from many sources—knowledge, status, organization, position, force, charisma, convictions, money, time, the accident of birth, and conflict.

The resources of the initiators must be enlarged during this third stage of the change process to include the persons who have the power to turn an idea into reality. Who these holders of power are and their sources of power will vary from issue to issue. Ed Brown, for example, soon realized that if anything was to be done in the West End Allotment, he needed the support of the mayor. By virtue of his position the mayor could provide, or withhold, support that could be decisive in the change process. In the rural Wisconsin church the

Sunday school teachers gained a high degree of power for themselves simply by organizing and presenting a firm, united front. They also sought and secured the support of the powerful official board of the church.

As was pointed out earlier, the individual who is experienced in the process of planned change will have foreseen the eventual need for legitimation and power. Therefore in fanning the embers of discontent and in widening the circle of initiators, he will have been careful to keep the channels of communication open to those who can supply the needed stamp of approval and to the holders of power. In short, he foresees the eventual need to build a consensus in support of change.

On the one hand the search for a consensus means maximizing the number and variety of supporters. On the other hand, it also means neutralizing potential opposition. Both require an awareness of the "rule of reciprocity." Frequently potential opponents of a program can be turned into supporters of change simply by including them in the planning process. This is what happened in the West End Allotment. If a group of outsiders had gone ahead on their own in developing a plan to improve the housing in that area, they almost certainly would have been opposed by a large number of the residents who would have been suspicious of any plan to displace them from their homes. By including residents in the planning group, this potential opposition was eliminated, and the planning process was enriched by the ideas and suggestions of the residents.

On the other hand the initiating group completely neglected the local realty association, and the subsequent opposition of this group almost killed the plan. Frequently, care in discussing the proposal for change with all interested persons can neutralize potential opposition; sometimes other efforts are required, and these may require invoking the rule of reciprocity. "If you'll help us, or at least not oppose this plan, then I'll help you on the proposal you've been talking about."

Development of an Executing Group

This third step of building a coalition in support of the proposal for change leads directly into the fourth step, the development of an *executing group*. In the rural Wisconsin church the executing group consisted of a building committee, the architect, and the contractor. Here, as is so often the case, it was necessary to call in specialists to help execute the plan. In this case the "outside" experts were the architects and the contractor.

When the coalition put together by Ed Brown and the Social Action Committee at Westminster Church finally was able to agree on a program they could all support, they found they needed several different kinds of professional skills in the execution stage. The program called for the city to establish a housing authority which would build and operate an eighty-eight-unit public housing project; it called for the preparation and implementation of an urban renewal program which included the rehabilitation of forty-six homes in the West End Allotment; and it included a provision that enabled twenty-nine low-income families to buy homes with 100 percent mortgages at 3 percent interest. The referendum authorizing the city to undertake this venture would not have passed without the assistance of some highly skilled public relations specialists. The implementation of this program required the assistance of urban renewal consultants, housing experts, and bankers.

Institutionalizing Change

Many efforts at planned change eventually turn out to be less successful than was originally anticipated. One of the most common reasons for this is that as the enthusiasm of the initiating group wears thin, there is no one pushing for the detailed implementation of the program. The most effective method of preventing this is to institutionalize the program. What began as a citizen's movement to "do something" about housing conditions in the West End Allotment became institutionalized when the city government accepted responsibility for actual implementation of the program. The newly created housing authority, which included both Ed Brown and the pastor of Westminster Church as board members, had the authority, the institutional stability, and the continuity necessary to see the program through to its conclusion.

By contrast a common example of what happens when a program is not institutionalized can be seen in cooperative ministries. Every year in scores of communities churchmen get together and share their *discontent* about the ineffectiveness of their local churches, which have been operating unilaterally, to deal satisfactorily with certain common concerns. Frequently a few leaders will take the *initiative* and propose formation of a group ministry or a larger parish. They successfully enlist the *support* of others for their plan, and the new cooperative ministry is formally launched with considerable local publicity. The initiating group believes that their program has been accepted and *implemented*.

After the passage of several months, or perhaps a year or two, it often becomes apparent to everyone that the cooperative ministry is not living up to expectations. Some of the laymen are diverted by new responsibilities in their own congregations, or perhaps the minister who was the strongest advocate of the idea moves away, and the original enthusiasm fades. Often no one is able to point to the exact date when it happened, but a few years later everyone agrees that this particular venture in interchurch cooperation has ended.

An analysis of the venture usually reveals that it died because it was not institutionalized. It lacked the institutional structure required for continuity and detailed implementation of all the original plans. This is not necessarily bad; many local church programs should be terminated after the point of diminishing returns has been reached, and this includes some programs of interchurch cooperation. On the other hand, however, many cooperative ministries have continued to function for years and have been extremely valuable. Usually these become highly institutionalized operations with a clearly designated leader, a distinctive identity, an adequate budget, and a board or council of dedicated individuals with a high degree of loyalty to the group. Thus when there is a change in leadership or in program emphasis, the built-in institutional strength of the organization enables the ministry to continue through what becomes only a transition phase rather than a termination point.

Conclusion

The strategy for planned change outlined in this chapter can be used in a variety of situations. It can be helpful to the citizen who believes the curriculum in the local schools should be enriched. It can be utilized by the group of ministers who want to develop a chaplaincy program in their community for the hospitals, the county jail, the several nursing homes, and the new apartment tower for "golden-agers." It can guide the efforts of the new church school superintendent who wants to broaden the Christian education program in his church. It can be the outline for action by the group who believe the future for old First Church can be even more significant than its rich past has been. It can be the format for a new thrust for social justice in the community.

This book began with a chapter emphasizing the importance of the search for purpose by Christians who are concerned about the role and the relevancy of their local church. Following this were chapters discussing specific planning problems encountered by local churches as they look toward the future. In each of these the reader might ask: But how do we go about making those changes and adaptations required by a new day and a new challenge? The outline for a strategy for change presented in this chapter is one approach to answering this question.

Suggestions for Further Reading

Allen, Roland. *The Spontaneous Expansion of the Church.*
Grand Rapids: Wm. B. Eerdmans Publishing Company,
1962.

Barr, Browne. *Parish Back Talk.* Nashville: Abingdon Press,
1964.

Brunner, Emil. *The Understanding of the Church.* London:
Lutterworth Press, 1952.

Clark, M. Edward *et al.,* eds. *The Church Creative.* Nashville:
Abingdon Press, 1967.

Douglass, H. Paul. *1000 City Churches.* New York: George
H. Doran Company, 1926.

Fisher, Wallace E. *From Tradition to Mission.* Nashville:
Abingdon Press, 1965.

Gardner, E. Clinton. *The Church as a Prophetic Community.*
Philadelphia: The Westminster Press, 1967.

Grimes, Howard. *The Church Redemptive.* Nashville: Abingdon Press, 1958.

Judy, Marvin. *The Cooperative Parish in Nonmetropolitan Areas.* Nashville: Abingdon Press, 1967.

Leiffer, Murray H. *The Effective City Church.* 2nd rev. ed. Nashville: Abingdon Press, 1961.

Moberg, David O. *The Church as a Social Institution.* Englewood Cliffs: Prentice-Hall, 1962.

Moore, Richard E., and Day, D. L. *Urban Church Breakthrough.* New York: Harper & Row, 1966.

Schaller, Lyle E. *Planning for Protestantism in Urban America.* Nashville: Abingdon Press, 1965.

Shippey, Frederick A. *Protestantism in Suburban Life.* Nashville: Abingdon Press, 1964.

Sills, Horace S., ed. *Grassroots Ecumenicity.* Philadelphia: United Church Press, 1967.

Trueblood, Elton. *The Company of the Committed.* New York: Harper & Row, 1961.

Weller, Jack E. *Yesterday's People: Life in Contemporary Appalachia.* Lexington: University of Kentucky Press, 1965.